D1142960

APM Competence Framework

APM Competence Framework

Association for Project Management

Association for Project Management
150 West Wycombe Road
High Wycombe
Buckinghamshire
HP12 3AE

©Association for Project Management 2008

All rights reserved. No part of this publication may be reproduced, stored in a retrieval system or transmitted, in any form or by any means, without the express permission in writing of the Chief Executive of the Association for Project Management. Within the United Kingdom exceptions are allowed in respect of fair dealing for the purposes of research or private study, or criticism or review, as permitted under the Copyright, Designs and Patents Act, 1988, and its amendments, or in the case of reprographic reproduction in accordance with the terms of the licences issued by the appropriate reprographic rights organisations, such as the Copyright Licensing Agency. Enquiries concerning reproduction outside these terms and in other countries should be sent to the Publishing Rights Department, Association for Project Management, at the address above.

Readers are responsible for the correct application of the information in this publication and its conformity with all relevant legal and commercial obligations. The Association for Project Management cannot accept legal responsibility or liability for any errors or omissions in the book or the consequences thereof.

All registered trademarks are hereby acknowledged and the publisher makes no claim to these trademarks.

British Library Cataloguing in Publication Data is available
ISBN 10: 1-903494-18-4
ISBN 13: 978-1-903494-18-9

Cover design by Fountainhead
Typeset by RefineCatch
Printed by Hobbs the Printers Ltd, Totton, Hampshire
Copy editor Merle Read
Proofreader Patrick Cole
Publishing Manager Ingmar Folkmans

CONTENTS

Contents

FIGURES AND TABLES

FIGURES

TABLES

FOREWORD

As Chairman of the Association for Project Management, recognised as a leading, world-class organisation furthering the development of the project management profession, I welcome you to this first edition of its project management competence framework.

Linked to the *APM Body of Knowledge* (5th edition) and the *ICB-International Project Management Association Competence Baseline* (3rd edition), this document provides a clear and simple guide to the range of individual competences in project management. It represents an essential part of the toolkit for all professional project managers, allowing them to assess and develop their competences and those of their teams.

Based on wide consultation among leading practitioners, this is a valuable tool for assessing current knowledge and experience, identifying training and development needs, and evaluating an individual's readiness to obtain the appropriate internationally recognised professional qualifications. Designed to be extremely user-friendly, the *APM Competence Framework* provides specific measures for the knowledge and experience which need to be maintained and nurtured through continuing professional development.

Many UK organisations have developed, or are in the process of developing, their own project management competence frameworks to meet their specific organisational needs. This APM document provides an ideal means of benchmarking organisation-specific frameworks to the international standards and qualifications of a much broader global community.

I commend to you the *APM Competence Framework*, as I am confident it will benefit you, your organisation and indeed all sectors of the economy in the crucial quest to enhance project management capability.

Mike Nichols
Chairman of the APM

INTRODUCTION

1.1 OVERVIEW

This competence framework has been developed by the Association for Project Management (APM) using the knowledge and experience of project management practitioners from across UK industry and academia, coupled with thorough research of a variety of competence frameworks worldwide in the area of project management. It has been designed to support the project management community by defining the competence elements needed for effective project management across three domains: technical, behavioural and contextual. It is used by the APM, along with the *APM Body of Knowledge* (5th edition, 2006), to support its membership, professional development and knowledge services.

The *APM Body of Knowledge* and the *ICB-International Project Management Association [IPMA] Competence Baseline* (version 3.0) provided the foundation for the *APM Competence Framework*. The framework, represented by a 'wheel of competence', has also greatly benefited from the feedback and contributions provided by practising project managers at all levels.

The *APM Competence Framework* defines the work of project management personnel, and allows for the identification and classification of the different competence elements needed for effective project management by project managers at all levels. The competence framework sets out the 30 technical, nine behavioural and eight contextual competence elements required of an effective project manager.

The APM has defined four Levels of Competence (Levels D to A) which are aligned to the IPMA four-level structure. The same competence elements apply at all Levels, but knowledge and experience should grow deeper and broader from APM Level D to Level A.

The *APM Competence Framework* is useful for the identification of appropriate qualifications and for the benefit of those interested in project management skills and personal development.

1.1.1 Competence

A competence articulates the expected outcome or performance standard that is achieved as a result of applying a combination of knowledge, personal attitude, and skills and experience in a certain function. It can be understood to represent the language of performance in an organisation, articulating both the expected outcomes of an individual's efforts and the manner in which these activities are carried out.

1.2 BENEFITS OF A COMPETENCE FRAMEWORK

Significant benefits can be derived from using an approved competence framework, both for the professional and for the organisations that employ them. From the perspective of the individual project manager, the primary benefits of using the *APM Competence Framework* are that it ensures a common understanding of the competences required of them; that it enables them to assess their competence levels against a framework aligned with an agreed international standard; and that it helps them to identify areas for development and judge their readiness for attainment of professional qualifications and certifications.

From the employers' perspective, the framework enables them to come to a judgement about the PM competence of employees at all levels, assessed against an internationally agreed standard; to analyse overall strengths and weaknesses; and to identify corporate training and developmental needs. It can relieve organisations of the need to develop and maintain their own PM competence framework or, alternatively, it can provide the core for a more tailored solution, if required.

Many individuals and organisations will recognise the very significant benefits they can derive from exploiting aspects of the competence framework, but for them using it in its entirety may not be practical or appropriate. In designing the framework the APM has been mindful of this, and guidance on how it can be adapted to meet differing needs is set out in Appendix 2.

1.3 THE APM WHEEL OF COMPETENCE

1.3.1 Defining the wheel of competence

The wheel of competence (as shown in Figure 1.1 overleaf) represents the integration of all the competence elements required of an effective project manager. The competence elements are grouped into the relevant competence domains, of which there are three: technical, behavioural and contextual. Additionally, at the centre of the wheel lie the five key concepts which refer to the environment within which a project is undertaken. The wheel signifies that projects are managed in a dynamic, fast-changing environment, and hence the need for ongoing self-assessment and continuous professional development.

1.4 KEY CONCEPTS

There are five key concepts which form the foundation for the *APM Competence Framework*. These concepts refer to the environment within which a project is undertaken: projects do not exist in a vacuum. A project will be managed differently according to a wide range of factors, both internal and external to the organisation – for example, organisational capability and maturity or legal and technical factors (for more detail refer to the *APM Body of Knowledge*, 5th edn).

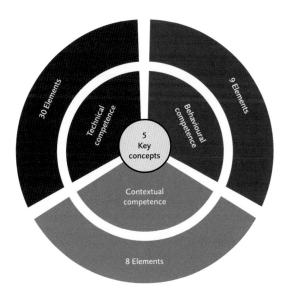

Figure 1.1 *The wheel of competence*

KC01 Project management. Project management is the process by which projects are defined, planned, monitored, controlled and delivered such that agreed benefits are realised. Projects are unique, transient endeavours undertaken to achieve a desired outcome. Projects bring about change, and project management is recognised as the most efficient way of managing such change.

KC02 Programme management. Programme management is the coordinated management of related projects, which may include related business-as-usual activities that together achieve a beneficial change of a strategic nature for an organisation. What constitutes a programme will vary across industries and business sectors, but there are core programme management processes.

KC03 Portfolio management. Portfolio management is the selection and management of all of an organisation's projects, programmes and related business-as-usual activities, taking into account resource constraints. A portfolio is a group of projects and programmes carried out under the sponsorship of an organisation. Portfolios can be managed at an organisational, programme or functional level.

KC04 Project context. Project context refers to the environment within which a project is undertaken. Projects do not exist in a vacuum, and an appreciation of the context within which the project is being performed will assist those involved in project management to deliver a project.

KC05 Project office. A project office serves the organisation's project management needs. A project office can range from simple support functions for the project manager to responsibility for linking corporate strategy to project execution.

1.5 THE THREE DOMAINS

The technical, behavioural and contextual competences are outlined in Table 1.1. on page 5.

1.5.1 Technical competence elements

The **technical competence domain** contains the functional project management competence elements. The scope of **technical competences** includes the elements relating to:

- the delivery of projects, programmes and portfolios;
- the integration of work in any temporary project, programme and portfolio organisation;
- the production of project deliverables in the project organisation;
- the progress through all phases of the project, all stages of a programme and all periods of the portfolio considered.

The *APM Competence Framework* contains 30 technical competence elements.

1.5.2 Behavioural competence elements

The **behavioural competence domain** contains the personal project management competence elements, covering attitudes and skills. The scope of **behavioural competences** includes the elements relating to:

- the project manager specifically;
- the project manager's relationship with direct contacts in and around the project;
- the project manager's interaction with the whole project and parties involved;
- the project manager's interaction with the broader environment, such as the political, economical, sociological, cultural and historical context.

The *APM Competence Framework* contains nine behavioural competence elements.

1.5.3 Contextual competence elements

The **contextual competence domain** contains the organisational competence elements. The scope of **contextual competences** includes elements relating to:

- the role of project management in permanent organisations;
- the interrelationship between project management and the organisation's business functions and administration.

The *APM Competence Framework* contains eight contextual competence elements.

Table 1.1 *Overview of the competence elements*

Technical competence (TC)		Behavioural competence (BC)		Contextual competence (CC)	
TC01	Concept	BC01	Communication	CC01	Project sponsorship
TC02	Project success and benefits management	BC02	Teamwork	CC02	Health, safety and environmental management
TC03	Stakeholder management	BC03	Leadership	CC03	Project life cycles
TC04	Requirements management	BC04	Conflict management	CC04	Project finance and funding
TC05	Project risk management	BC05	Negotiation	CC05	Legal awareness
TC06	Estimating	BC06	Human resource management	CC06	Organisational roles
TC07	Business case	BC07	Behavioural characteristics	CC07	Organisation structure
TC08	Marketing and sales	BC08	Learning and development	CC08	Governance of project management
TC09	Project reviews	BC09	Professionalism and ethics		
TC10	Definition				
TC11	Scope management				
TC12	Modelling and testing				
TC13	Methods and procedures				
TC14	Project quality management				
TC15	Scheduling				
TC16	Resource management				
TC17	Information management and reporting				
TC18	Project management plan				
TC19	Configuration management				
TC20	Change control				
TC21	Implementation				
TC22	Technology management				
TC23	Budgeting and cost management				
TC24	Procurement				
TC25	Issue management				
TC26	Development				
TC27	Value management				
TC28	Earned value management				
TC29	Value engineering				
TC30	Handover and closeout				

1.6 APM LEVELS OF COMPETENCE

Each competence element takes its definition from the *APM Body of Knowledge* (5th edn), and has a number of indicators to facilitate the assessment of competence against the element. The knowledge and experience required at each APM Level is described in key Competence Level statements.

In this *APM Competence Framework*, the following four Levels of Competence are specified:

- projects director (APM Level A)
- senior project manager (APM Level B)
- project manager (APM Level C)
- project management associate (APM Level D)

The Level of Competence required at each APM Level increases as the requisite knowledge and experience of the individual broadens and deepens.

1.6.1 APM Level A

The projects director will have at least five years of experience in portfolio management, programme management or multi-project management, of which three years were in responsible leadership functions in the portfolio management of a company/organisation or a business unit, or in the management of important programmes.

The project director:

- shall be able to manage portfolios or programmes;
- is responsible for the management of an important portfolio of a company/organisation or a branch thereof, or for the management of one or more important programmes;
- contributes to strategic management and makes proposals to senior management;
- develops project management personnel and coaches project managers;
- develops and implements project management requirements, processes, methods, techniques, tools, handbooks and guidelines.

1.6.2 APM Level B

The senior project manager will have at least five years of project management experience, of which three years were in responsible leadership functions of complex projects.

The senior project manager:

- shall be able to manage complex projects;
- is responsible for all project management competence elements of a complex project;

- has a general management role as manager of a large project management team;
- uses adequate project management processes, methods, techniques and tools.

1.6.3 APM Level C

The project manager will have at least three years of project management experience and is responsible for leadership functions of projects with limited complexity.

The project manager:

- shall be able to manage projects with limited complexity, and/or to manage the sub-project of a complex project in all competence elements of project management;
- is responsible for managing a project with limited complexity in all its aspects, or for managing a sub-project of a complex project;
- applies common project management processes, methods, techniques and tools.

1.6.4 APM Level D

It is not compulsory for a project management associate to have experience in the project management competence elements, but it is an advantage if the candidate has already applied their project management knowledge to some extent already.

A project management associate:

- shall have project management knowledge in all required competence elements;
- can practise in any project management competence element;
- may work in some fields as a specialist;
- works as a project team member or a member of the project personnel;
- has broad project management knowledge and the ability to apply it.

1.7 DEGREES OF COMPETENCE

The **degree of competence** is defined by general descriptions of knowledge and experience, and evaluated on a scale from 0 to 10 as shown in Table 1.2 (the extreme values of the scale are rarely used in real assessments). Defined scores for each competence (based on the assessment of knowledge and experience against the above scale) for each APM Level (D to A) have been determined.

Table 1.2 *Competence indicator scoring matrix*

Score	KNOWLEDGE	Score	EXPERIENCE
0	None	0	None
Low – Limited knowledge/experience In knowledge terms: the candidate knows the element and is able to present and explain known criteria for this element. In experience terms: the candidate has some experience obtained from a project management role in a few projects in one sector of the economy or unit of an organisation during one or several phases of these projects.			
1	Has an awareness of the competence element.	1	Has participated in a single project which involved the competence element.
2	Knows about the competence element.	2	Has participated in a number of projects which have involved the competence element.
3	Can describe the competence element.	3	Has practised the competence element with others in a number of projects.
Medium – Significant knowledge/experience In knowledge terms: the candidate has a solid level of knowledge and is able to recognise and to apply the relevant criteria, as well as check the results. In experience terms: the candidate has experience and a track record obtained from applying many project management competences across several projects in at least one sector of the economy during most phases of these projects.			
4	Has an understanding of how the competence element could be practised within a single project.	4	Has independently practised the competence element in a number of projects.
5	Has an understanding of how the competence element could be practised within a number of projects and can evaluate the value to the projects.	5	Has managed others practising the competence element in a number of projects.
6	Has a good understanding of how the competence element could be practised within a complex project and can evaluate and adapt as required.	6	Has managed others practising the competence element in a complex project.
High – Extensive knowledge/experience In knowledge terms: the candidate understands the role in detail and is able to evaluate, to create and to integrate the relevant criteria and can interpret and evaluate the results. In experience terms: the candidate has a broad range of experience and a good track record gained from responsible project management roles in many different kinds of projects across one or more industry sectors, during most or all phases of these projects.			
7	Has a detailed understanding of how the competence element is practised within complex projects and can critically evaluate and optimise as required.	7	Has managed others practising the competence element in a number of complex projects.
8	Has a detailed understanding of how the competence element is practised within complex projects and can critically evaluate and develop further as required.	8	Has managed others practising the competence element in many complex projects.
9	Has a deep knowledge of how the competence element is practised within very complex projects and can educate others.	9	Has guided and facilitated others in practising the competence element in very complex projects.
10	Has a deep knowledge of all aspects of the competence element in very complex projects and is a recognised industry expert (written papers and presentations).	10	Has guided and facilitated others in all aspects of the competence element in very complex projects and is a recognised industry expert.

Although the scores vary from competence to competence, the average scores for knowledge and experience are as shown in Table 1.3. The knowledge and experience requirements become deeper (from knowing the facts to developing the ability to apply and evaluate methods, and so on) and broader (from one to several different kinds of projects, methods, and so on) from Level D to Level A.

Table 1.3 *Knowledge and experience average scores required at each APM Level of Competence*

Level of Competence	APM Level D	APM Level C	APM Level B	APM Level A
Knowledge	4	5	6	7
Experience	0/Optional	4	6	7
Average	4	4.5	6	7

Overall competence is based on a number of competences, so individuals will have a range of scores. The overlapping ranges for each APM Level are as shown in Figure 1.2. Note: there is a minimum score (for each competence) required for each APM Level. So, even though an individual may have a score equivalent to a Level B in one or more competences, if the average across the group of competences is 4.5 or an individual competence has a score of 4 or less, the person is classed as being at APM Level C.

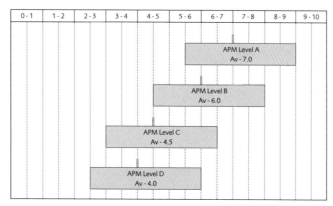

Figure 1.2 *Usual range and average scores for each APM Competence Level*

Appendix 6 shows the relationship between the scores required for each competency and the APM Levels.

1.8 COMPLEXITY OF PROJECTS

In order to determine Levels of Competence of project managers, the complexity of the challenges to which they have had exposure must be considered. In the previous section, the higher Competence Levels are characterised by involvement in 'complex projects'. For these Levels of Competence to have meaning, it is important that the concept of project complexity is clearly understood. The APM considers that for a project to be considered 'complex' it would need to score highly against the following indicators/criteria (not in priority order):

- objectives, assessment of results;
- interested parties, integration;
- cultural and social context;
- degree of innovation, general conditions;
- project structure, demand for coordination;
- project organisation;
- leadership, teamwork, decisions;
- resources, including finance;
- risks and opportunities;
- project management methods, tools and techniques.

In a complex project environment, the project manager will need to take account of many interrelated subsystems/sub-projects and other elements, both within the structures of the project and in the wider organisation. A complex project is likely to involve interaction with several organisations and/or different units in the same organisation – these either benefiting from or providing resources to such a project. A complex project will typically comprise several different, sometimes overlapping, phases, and its effective management will require the coordination of the work of several different disciplines, as well as the use of a wide range of project management methods, tools and techniques.

An individual's experience of complexity may have been gained on more than one project, but the currency of any such experience obtained more than five years ago will be limited and should, in most circumstances, be discounted. Appendix 3 contains a tool used in the APM Level B certification process, which may be helpful in determining the level of complexity of any given project.

1.9 COMPLETING THE SELF-ASSESSMENT

1.9.1 Considerations

When undertaking self-assessment, it is understood that you may not wish to undertake assessment against all competence elements each time you use the competence framework. You may want to focus on only a selection of relevant competence elements at any particular time; however, over time the professional project manager will need to assess against all elements. Guidance on tailoring the framework can be found in Appendix 2.

In planning your assessment you will need to allow up to five minutes for completion of each competence element. The complexity of the projects you have worked on should be taken into account. You should refer to the complexity matrix in Appendix 3 to assess the complexity level of your specific projects.

1.9.2 Structure of competence elements

An example of a completed self-assessment summary for the technical competence domain is shown in Figure 1.3.

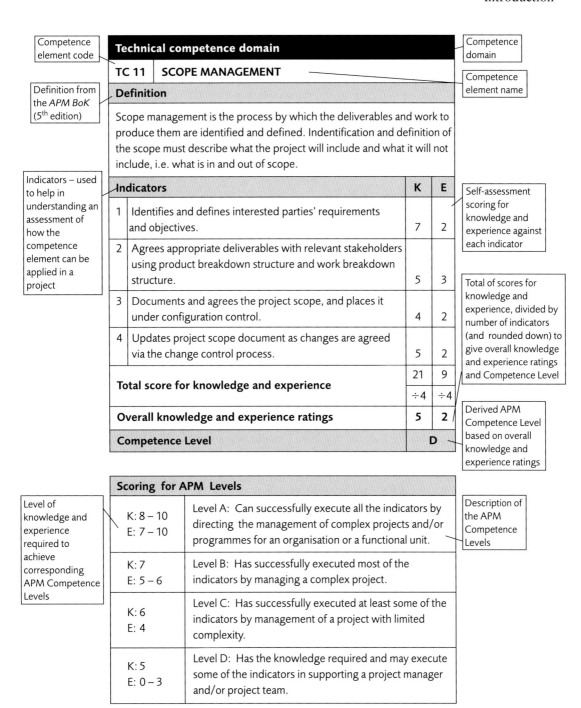

Figure 1.3 *Self-assessment example*

The labels surrounding the figure read:

Competence element code

Definition from the *APM BoK* (5th edition)

Indicators – used to help in understanding an assessment of how the competence element can be applied in a project

Level of knowledge and experience required to achieve corresponding APM Competence Levels

Competence domain

Competence element name

Self-assessment scoring for knowledge and experience against each indicator

Total of scores for knowledge and experience, divided by number of indicators (and rounded down) to give overall knowledge and experience ratings and Competence Level

Derived APM Competence Level based on overall knowledge and experience ratings

Description of the APM Competence Levels

Technical competence domain

TC 11	SCOPE MANAGEMENT

Definition

Scope management is the process by which the deliverables and work to produce them are identified and defined. Indentification and definition of the scope must describe what the project will include and what it will not include, i.e. what is in and out of scope.

Indicators		K	E
1	Identifies and defines interested parties' requirements and objectives.	7	2
2	Agrees appropriate deliverables with relevant stakeholders using product breakdown structure and work breakdown structure.	5	3
3	Documents and agrees the project scope, and places it under configuration control.	4	2
4	Updates project scope document as changes are agreed via the change control process.	5	2
Total score for knowledge and experience		21	9
		÷4	÷4
Overall knowledge and experience ratings		5	2
Competence Level		D	

Scoring for APM Levels		
K: 8 – 10 E: 7 – 10	Level A: Can successfully execute all the indicators by directing the management of complex projects and/or programmes for an organisation or a functional unit.	
K: 7 E: 5 – 6	Level B: Has successfully executed most of the indicators by managing a complex project.	
K: 6 E: 4	Level C: Has successfully executed at least some of the indicators by management of a project with limited complexity.	
K: 5 E: 0 – 3	Level D: Has the knowledge required and may execute some of the indicators in supporting a project manager and/or project team.	

11

1.9.3 Instructions for completing self-assessment

Step 1. Unfold front cover to reveal competence indicator scoring matrix and familiarise yourself with the scoring criteria. Unfold the back cover to reveal the self-assessment summary sheet.

Step 2. The competence indicator scoring matrix refers to complex projects. Go to the project complexity matrix (Appendix 3) and rate the complexity of your project(s) prior to beginning the assessment.

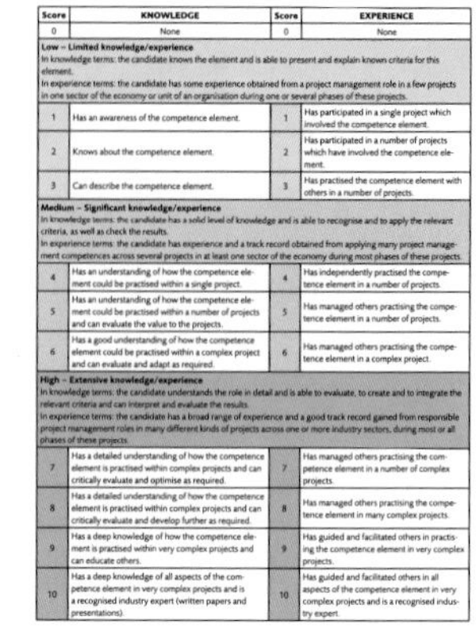

Figure 1.4 *Competence indicator scoring matrix*

Technical competence

Step 3. Go to the first **technical competence** (Chapter 2) to be assessed.

Step 4. For each indicator, assess yourself for both knowledge and experience on a scale of 1–10, using the competence indicator scoring matrix. Record your scores against each indicator for knowledge and experience in the appropriate column (K and E).

Step 5. When all indicators have been assessed for a competence, add up the scores in each column and enter the totals for the two columns (K and E).

Step 6. Calculate your 'overall knowledge and experience ratings' by dividing the totals by the number of indicators, and enter these figures in the appropriate boxes. Anything that is not a whole number should be rounded down – e.g. 3.9 rounded down to 3.

Step 7. Referring to the 'Scoring for APM Levels' guidance, determine the APM Level to which your score equates (A, B, C or D) and enter this in the 'Competence Level' box. Where your competence ranges across more than one APM Level, the lowest APM Level applies.

Step 8. Transfer your APM Competence Level (A, B, C or D) to the relevant line on the assessment summary sheet.

Repeat steps 3 to 8 for each of the remaining technical competences to be assessed.

Behavioural competence

Step 9. Repeat steps 3 to 8 for each **behavioural competence** (Chapter 3).

Figure 1.5 *Self-assessment summary sheet*

Contextual competence

Step 10. Repeat steps 3 to 8 for each **contextual competence** (Chapter 4).

1.9.4 Calculating your overall rating

Once the assessment is complete, you will have a clear picture of your score (in terms of knowledge and experience), and your overall competence rating for each competence in terms of APM Levels D to A.

For an overall rating, it is necessary to have a score against a significant grouping of competences: for example, all those associated with a specific organisational role – your organisation may decide to group specific competences and map them to job role definitions. The job role will define what you are required to score against these competences, such as Level B on 15 competences, in order to be a senior project manager in that organisation.

To work out your overall rating, review the range of scores and the average score across all the competences measured. The overall APM Level can be determined from Figure 1.2. Further guidance is given in section 1.7.

1.9.5 Identifying further development opportunities

In order to identify where further development is required, you will be able to drill down into the detail for each competence, looking at your competence score for each separate indicator, thus making it possible to identify the gaps in your knowledge and experience, for each competence, at your APM Level. This will provide useful information for discussion at personal development reviews and a road map for future training requirements and for your continuing professional development.

THE TECHNICAL COMPETENCE DOMAIN

The technical competence elements described here are needed through the full life cycle of concept, definition, implementation, and handover and closeout (Figure 2.1). However, the order in which a project manager may apply the competences can differ depending on the project type, size and complexity and other influencing factors. The importance or weight of a competence is completely dependent upon the specific project situation.

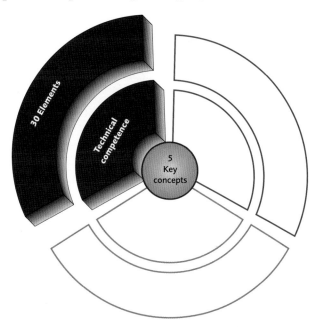

TC01	Concept	**TC11**	Scope management	**TC20**	Change control
TC02	Project success and benefits management	**TC12**	Modelling and testing	**TC21**	Implementation
		TC13	Methods and procedures	**TC22**	Technology management
TC03	Stakeholder management	**TC14**	Project quality management	**TC23**	Budgeting and cost management
TC04	Requirements management	**TC15**	Scheduling	**TC24**	Procurement
		TC16	Resource management	**TC25**	Issue management
TC05	Project risk management	**TC17**	Information management and reporting	**TC26**	Development
TC06	Estimating			**TC27**	Value management
TC07	Business case	**TC18**	Project management plan	**TC28**	Earned value management
TC08	Marketing and sales				
TC09	Project reviews	**TC19**	Configuration management	**TC29**	Value engineering
TC10	Definition			**TC30**	Handover and closeout

Figure 2.1 *The technical competence domain*

2.1 CONCEPT

Technical competence domain			
TC01	**CONCEPT**		
Definition			
Concept is the first phase in the project life cycle. During this phase the need, opportunity or problem is confirmed, the overall feasibility of the project is considered and a preferred solution identified. The business case for the project will be produced in this phase.			
Indicators		**K**	**E**
1	Gathers, documents and gets agreement on project requirements with key stakeholders.	6	4
2	Validates and/or develops a business case and project strategies, and places them under change management.	3	4
3	Defines project objectives, appraises the project (including financial appraisal), carries out feasibility study and establishes an outline project plan.	6	4
4	Identifies, assesses, documents and communicates the potential impact of high-level risks.		
5	Validates requirements at key points in the project life cycle.		
6	Assesses compliance with project objectives and requirements and seeks authorisation for the project.		
7	Gains approval either to progress to definition phase, refine concept phase or cancel project.		
8	Sets up project review process and associated schedule.		
Total score for knowledge and experience		÷8	÷8
Overall knowledge and experience ratings			
Competence Level			

Scoring for APM Levels	
K: 8–10 E: 7–10	Level A: Can successfully execute all the indicators by directing the management of complex projects and/or programmes for an organisation or a functional unit.
K: 7 E: 6	Level B: Has successfully executed most of the indicators by managing a complex project.
K: 6 E: 5	Level C: Has successfully executed at least some of the indicators by management of a project with limited complexity.
K: 5 E: 0–4	Level D: Has the knowledge required and may execute some of the indicators in supporting a project manager and/or project team.

2.2 PROJECT SUCCESS AND BENEFITS MANAGEMENT

Technical competence domain			
TC02	PROJECT SUCCESS AND BENEFITS MANAGEMENT		
Definition			
Project success is the satisfaction of stakeholder needs and is measured by the success criteria as identified and agreed at the start of the project. Benefits management is the identification of the benefits at an organisational level and the monitoring and realisation of those benefits.			
Indicators		**K**	**E**
1	Analyses and understands the project and its context within the proposed business change and how these can enable the expected benefits (indirect, direct, financial and non-financial).		
2	Agrees success criteria for the project with the sponsor, ensuring they are measurable.		
3	Agrees critical success factors for the project with stakeholders, ensuring they are measurable.		
4	Agrees KPIs, ensuring these are quantitative by using traditional time, cost and quality techniques.		
5	Understands the relationship between the timing of deliverables and the realisation of benefits.		
6	Discusses and agrees the project success criteria and benefits realisation responsibilities with all relevant stakeholders as part of the project management contract with the customer.		
7	Executes and controls PM plans and changes, and reports on project performance.		
8	Ensures that the impacts of any deviations from plan are considered against the business case and the benefits realisation plan, and are escalated to the responsible stakeholders.		
9	Collects results and prepares project performance reports against the agreed KPIs and anticipated benefits, and communicates to relevant stakeholders.		
10	Ensures that benchmark data is captured against which benefit realisation can be measured.		
Total score for knowledge and experience		÷10	÷10
Overall knowledge and experience ratings			
Competence Level			

Scoring for APM Levels	
K: 8–10 E: 8–10	Level A: Can successfully execute all the indicators by directing the management of complex projects and/or programmes for an organisation or a functional unit.
K: 7 E: 7	Level B: Has successfully executed most of the indicators by managing a complex project.
K: 6 E: 5–6	Level C: Has successfully executed at least some of the indicators by management of a project with limited complexity.
K: 4–5 E: 0–4	Level D: Has the knowledge required and may execute some of the indicators in supporting a project manager and/or project team.

2.3 STAKEHOLDER MANAGEMENT

Technical competence domain			
TC03	**STAKEHOLDER MANAGEMENT**		
Definition			
Stakeholder management is the systematic identification, analysis and planning of actions to communicate with, negotiate with and influence stakeholders. Stakeholders are all those who have an interest or role in the project or are impacted by the project.			
Indicators		**K**	**E**
1	Identifies and prioritises stakeholder interests.		
2	Analyses their interests, requirements and level of influence.		
3	Develops a strategy/plan to manage and communicates effectively with all stakeholders. Includes stakeholder interests and expectations in the requirements, objectives, scope, deliverables, time schedule and costs of the project plan.		
4	Implements and monitors the effectiveness of the stakeholder management plan.		
5	Communicates to stakeholders which of their requirements will be fulfilled or not fulfilled by the project.		
6	Ensures the threats and opportunities represented by stakeholders are captured and proactively managed as risks.		
7	Executes, communicates and manages changes in the stakeholder management plan throughout the life cycle.		
8	Gains the commitment of all stakeholders, including the most challenging.		
Total score for knowledge and experience			
		÷8	÷8
Overall knowledge and experience ratings			
Competence Level			

Scoring for APM Levels	
K: 8–10 E: 8–10	Level A: Can successfully execute all the indicators by directing the management of complex projects and/or programmes for an organisation or a functional unit.
K: 7 E: 7	Level B: Has successfully executed most of the indicators by managing a complex project.
K: 5–6 E: 5–6	Level C: Has successfully executed at least some of the indicators by management of a project with limited complexity.
K: 4 E: 0–4	Level D: Has the knowledge required and may execute some of the indicators in supporting a project manager and/or project team.

2.4 REQUIREMENTS MANAGEMENT

Technical competence domain		K	E
TC04	**REQUIREMENTS MANAGEMENT**		
Definition			
Requirements management is the process of capturing, analysing and testing the documented statement of stakeholder and user wants and needs. Requirements are a statement of the need that a project has to satisfy, and should be comprehensive, clear, well structured, traceable and testable.			
Indicators		**K**	**E**
1	Gathers, documents and gets agreement on project requirements and related acceptance criteria.		
2	Analyses and prioritises requirements, taking into consideration business benefits and priorities.		
3	Evaluates prioritised requirements to ensure they still meet the project objectives and will deliver the required benefits.		
4	Ensures documented requirements are subject to the project configuration management processes.		
5	Establishes a common understanding of the requirements across the project team and all stakeholders.		
Total score for knowledge and experience		$\div 5$	$\div 5$
Overall knowledge and experience ratings			
Competence Level			

Scoring for APM Levels	
K: 8–10 E: 7–10	Level A: Can successfully execute all the indicators by directing the management of complex projects and/or programmes for an organisation or a functional unit.
K: 7 E: 6	Level B: Has successfully executed most of the indicators by managing a complex project.
K: 6 E: 4–5	Level C: Has successfully executed at least some of the indicators by management of a project with limited complexity.
K: 5 E: 0–3	Level D: Has the knowledge required and may execute some of the indicators in supporting a project manager and/or project team.

2.5 PROJECT RISK MANAGEMENT

Technical competence domain		K	E
TC05	PROJECT RISK MANAGEMENT		
Definition			
Project risk management is a structured process that allows individual risk events and overall project risk to be understood and managed proactively, optimising project success by minimising threats and maximising opportunities.			
Indicators		**K**	**E**
1	Identifies and assesses risks and opportunities (using qualitative and quantitative techniques), including any assumptions, and prepares a risk log.		
2	Develops a risk and opportunity response plan, assigns ownership, and has it approved by the relevant body and communicated.		
3	Identifies and undertakes mitigation actions and formulates contingency plans as appropriate.		
4	Assesses the probability of achieving time, cost and quality objectives throughout the project.		
5	Continuously identifies new risks, reassesses risks, plans responses, modifies the project plan and updates the risk log.		
6	Facilitates risk workshops.		
Total score for knowledge and experience		÷6	÷6
Overall knowledge and experience ratings			
Competence Level			

Scoring for APM Levels	
K: 8–10 E: 7–10	Level A: Can successfully execute all the indicators by directing the management of complex projects and/or programmes for an organisation or a functional unit.
K: 7 E: 6	Level B: Has successfully executed most of the indicators by managing a complex project.
K: 6 E: 4–5	Level C: Has successfully executed at least some of the indicators by management of a project with limited complexity.
K: 5 E: 0–3	Level D: Has the knowledge required and may execute some of the indicators in supporting a project manager and/or project team.

2.6 ESTIMATING

Technical competence domain			
TC06	**ESTIMATING**		
Definition			
Estimating uses a range of tools and techniques to produce estimates. An estimate approximates project time and cost targets and is refined throughout the project life cycle.			
Indicators		**K**	**E**
1	Is aware of and understands the degrees of uncertainty that apply to estimates as they are developed throughout the project life cycle. Uses this knowledge to identify assumptions and risks to develop contingency proposals for the project.		
2	Depending on the type and needs of the project, ensures one or more of the three main estimating techniques (bottom-up, comparative and parametric) are used to prepare estimates.		
3	Ensures a suitable number of relevant experts are used to prepare estimates and that the resulting ranges of estimates are used to prepare an overall estimate, together with optimistic and pessimistic targets for each task.		
4	When using the bottom-up technique, develops product breakdown/work breakdown structures to identify the deliverables (products) and associated development activities needed.		
5	Ensures, whenever possible, that comparative techniques are used, e.g. estimates are based on previous experience and usage statistics.		
6	Uses the parametric technique where bottom-up is not feasible and/or comparative data is not available.		
7	Throughout the project ensures that estimates are continually reviewed and revised as and when new information becomes available and more is known about the project.		
Total score for knowledge and experience		÷7	÷7
Overall knowledge and experience ratings			
Competence Level			

Scoring for APM Levels	
K: 7–10 E: 7–10	Level A: Can successfully execute all the indicators by directing the management of complex projects and/or programmes for an organisation or a functional unit.
K: 6 E: 6	Level B: Has successfully executed most of the indicators by managing a complex project.
K: 5 E: 5	Level C: Has successfully executed at least some of the indicators by management of a project with limited complexity.
K: 1–4 E: 0–4	Level D: Has the knowledge required and may execute some of the indicators in supporting a project manager and/or project team.

2.7 BUSINESS CASE

Technical competence domain			
TC07	**BUSINESS CASE**		
Definition			
The business case provides justification for undertaking a project, in terms of evaluating the benefit, cost and risk of alternative options and rationale for the preferred solution. Its purpose is to obtain management commitment and approval for investment in the project. The business case is owned by the sponsor.			
Indicators		**K**	**E**
1	Understands the content and is prepared to write a business case on behalf of the sponsor according to the customer's standards and accounting norms.		
2	Is aware of the internal (i.e. project/programme changes) and external (legislative, market forces) factors that could impact the business case.		
3	Articulates the balance between the benefits sought and the costs and risks of delivering these benefits for each of the options identified.		
4	Ensures the project/programme team are made aware of the business case and the potential impact to the business case arising from any changes to the programme and/or associated project plans.		
5	Throughout the project/programme and at closure, evaluates against the business case to ensure the continued viability of the project/programme; reports and escalates any variations to appropriate management levels for decisions.		
Total score for knowledge and experience		÷5	÷5
Overall knowledge and experience ratings			
Competence Level			

Scoring for APM Levels	
K: 7–10 E: 7–10	Level A: Can successfully execute all the indicators by directing the management of complex projects and/or programmes for an organisation or a functional unit.
K: 6 E: 6	Level B: Has successfully executed most of the indicators by managing a complex project.
K: 5 E: 5	Level C: Has successfully executed at least some of the indicators by management of a project with limited complexity.
K: 1–4 E: 0–4	Level D: Has the knowledge required and may execute some of the indicators in supporting a project manager and/or project team.

2.8 MARKETING AND SALES

Technical competence domain		K	E
TC08	**MARKETING AND SALES**		
Definition			
Marketing involves anticipating the demands of users and identifying and satisfying their needs by providing the right project at the right time, cost and quality. Sales is a marketing technique used to promote a project. Marketing and sales needs to be undertaken internally and possibly externally to an organisation.			
Indicators		**K**	**E**
1	Develops marketing and sales strategy for the project.		
2	Ensures external and internal environment is understood in terms of project context in effective marketing strategy.		
3	Is aware of various selling techniques to achieve buy-in from stakeholders, the project team and users for the project's approach.		
4	Demonstrates appropriate negotiation and influencing skills in marketing and sales.		
5	Investigates and analyses customer dynamics and uses research to inform marketing plans.		
6	Is aware of the impact of marketing and sales in assisting and securing appropriate resources.		
7	Is aware of the need to draw on marketing expertise available within the project or organisation or externally for effective marketing and sales.		
8	Ensures conformance to any copyright, IPR or any other legal framework that applies to the project deliverables.		
9	Monitors and evaluates marketing and sales activities.		
Total score for knowledge and experience		÷9	÷9
Overall knowledge and experience ratings			
Competence Level			

Scoring for APM Levels	
K: 8–10 E: 7–10	Level A: Can successfully execute all the indicators by directing the management of complex projects and/or programmes for an organisation or a functional unit.
K: 6–7 E: 5–6	Level B: Has successfully executed most of the indicators by managing a complex project.
K: 5 E: 4	Level C: Has successfully executed at least some of the indicators by management of a project with limited complexity.
K: 1–4 E: 0–3	Level D: Has the knowledge required and may execute some of the indicators in supporting a project manager and/or project team.

2.9 PROJECT REVIEWS

Technical competence domain		K	E
TC09	**PROJECT REVIEWS**		
Definition			
Project reviews take place throughout the project life cycle to check the likely or actual achievement of the objectives specified in the project management plan (PMP) and the benefits detailed in the business case. Additional reviews will take place following handover and closeout to ensure that the benefits are being realised by the organisation.			
Indicators		**K**	**E**
1	Establishes an effective project review system to be used during and after the project is complete (post-project review).		
2	Schedules project evaluation reviews at key stages during the project.		
3	During each evaluation: <ul><li>evaluates the project management processes used</li><li>reviews the likely technical success of the project</li><li>reviews the likely commercial success of the project (e.g. does it still meet the business case?)</li><li>validates overall progress to time, cost and quality</li><li>considers stakeholder relationships and perceptions</li><li>develops and applies corrective actions.</li></ul>		
4	Reports project status and performance to interested parties and agrees resulting actions.		
5	At post-project review, prepares a lessons-learned report and applies to future projects.		
Total score for knowledge and experience			
		÷5	÷5
Overall knowledge and experience ratings			
Competence Level			

Scoring for APM Levels	
K: 8–10 E: 8–10	Level A: Can successfully execute all the indicators by directing the management of complex projects and/or programmes for an organisation or a functional unit.
K: 7 E: 6–7	Level B: Has successfully executed most of the indicators by managing a complex project.
K: 5–6 E: 4–5	Level C: Has successfully executed at least some of the indicators by management of a project with limited complexity.
K: 1–4 E: 0–3	Level D: Has the knowledge required and may execute some of the indicators in supporting a project manager and/or project team.

2.10 DEFINITION

Technical competence domain			
TC10	**DEFINITION**		
Definition			
Definition is the second phase of the project life cycle. During this phase the preferred solution is further evaluated and optimised. Often an iterative process, definition can affect requirements and the project's scope, time, cost and quality objectives. As part of this phase the project management plan (PMP) is produced and the resources required during the implementation phase will be identified.			
Indicators		**K**	**E**
1	Considers alternative designs, using modelling and what-if techniques to meet the preferred solution.		
2	Agrees a design and the preferred solution with the sponsor and stakeholders, ensuring that they can meet the conditions (especially the supply of resources) necessitated by the solution.		
3	Prepares a detailed PMP, incorporating: • risk management plan • quality plan • communication plan • health and safety plan (as required) • benefits management plan (or the project's contribution to it).		
4	Revalidates the estimates based on the design and risk mitigation.		
5	Communicates and updates the business with any changes from the concept phase.		
6	Finalises and agrees the PMP with the sponsor and stakeholders.		
7	Gains approval from the business to move the project to the implementation phase, refine the definition phase or cancel the project.		
Total score for knowledge and experience		÷7	÷7
Overall knowledge and experience ratings			
Competence Level			

Scoring for APM Levels	
K: 8–10 E: 7–10	Level A: Can successfully execute all the indicators by directing the management of complex projects and/or programmes for an organisation or a functional unit.
K: 7 E: 5–6	Level B: Has successfully executed most of the indicators by managing a complex project.
K: 6 E: 4	Level C: Has successfully executed at least some of the indicators by management of a project with limited complexity.
K: 1–5 E: 0–3	Level D: Has the knowledge required and may execute some of the indicators in supporting a project manager and/or project team.

2.11 SCOPE MANAGEMENT

Technical competence domain			
TC11	**SCOPE MANAGEMENT**		
Definition			
Scope management is the process by which the deliverables and work to produce them are identified and defined. Identification and definition of the scope must describe what the project will include and what it will not include, i.e. what is in and out of scope.			
Indicators		**K**	**E**
1	Identifies and defines interested parties' requirements and objectives.		
2	Agrees appropriate deliverables with relevant stakeholders using product breakdown structure and work breakdown structure.		
3	Documents and agrees the project scope, and places it under configuration control.		
4	Updates project scope document as changes are agreed via the change control process.		
Total score for knowledge and experience		÷4	÷4
Overall knowledge and experience ratings			
Competence Level			

Scoring for APM Levels	
K: 8–10 E: 7–10	Level A: Can successfully execute all the indicators by directing the management of complex projects and/or programmes for an organisation or a functional unit.
K: 7 E: 5–6	Level B: Has successfully executed most of the indicators by managing a complex project.
K: 6 E: 4	Level C: Has successfully executed at least some of the indicators by management of a project with limited complexity.
K: 5 E: 0–3	Level D: Has the knowledge required and may execute some of the indicators in supporting a project manager and/or project team.

2.12 MODELLING AND TESTING

Technical competence domain		K	E
TC12	**MODELLING AND TESTING**		
Definition			
Modelling and testing are used to provide a representation and assurance of whether the project objectives can be achieved. Modelling is the process of creating and using a device that duplicates the physical or operational aspects of a deliverable. Testing is the process of determining how aspects of a deliverable perform when subjected to specified conditions.			
Indicators		**K**	**E**
1	Identifies project deliverables that require prototyping, modelling and/or testing.		
2	Develops an appropriate testing strategy and schedule, agrees them with the sponsor and stakeholders, and ensures incorporation in project schedule.		
3	Ensures that project plans take account of areas of uncertainty, identifying responsibilities and allowing adequate budget and time for resolution.		
4	Ensures that the design decisions taken at one stage are based on information discovered in earlier stages.		
5	Ensures that a robust and logical approach is adopted and applied in generating and managing technical, cost and schedule risk associated with modelling and testing.		
6	Ensures that modelling and testing are an integral part of quality assurance and quality control.		
Total score for knowledge and experience		$\div 6$	$\div 6$
Overall knowledge and experience ratings			
Competence Level			

Scoring for APM Levels	
K: 7–10 E: 6–10	Level A: Can successfully execute all the indicators by directing the management of complex projects and/or programmes for an organisation or a functional unit.
K: 5–6 E: 4–5	Level B: Has successfully executed most of the indicators by managing a complex project.
K: 4 E: 3	Level C: Has successfully executed at least some of the indicators by management of a project with limited complexity.
K: 1–3 E: 0–2	Level D: Has the knowledge required and may execute some of the indicators in supporting a project manager and/or project team.

2.13 METHODS AND PROCEDURES

Technical competence domain			
TC13	METHODS AND PROCEDURES		
Definition			
Methods and procedures detail the standard practices to be used for managing projects throughout a life cycle. Methods provide a consistent framework within which project management is performed. Procedures cover individual aspects of project management practice and form an integral part of a method.			
Indicators		K	E
1	Understands the organisation's project and programme management methods, processes and supporting systems, including appropriate delivery life cycles available for use by the project.		
2	Complements the organisation's methods and procedures through the use of recognised project and/or programme management techniques, tools and experience, and scales these appropriately to the complexity and risk requirements of the project/programme.		
3	Ensures the methods and procedures adopted integrate into the organisation's reporting structure and schedule.		
4	Ensures all members of the project team understand the methods and procedures to be employed, using training and/or coaching as necessary.		
5	Ensures improvements developed on the project are communicated and offered as general improvements to the organisation's methods and procedures.		
Total score for knowledge and experience		÷5	÷5
Overall knowledge and experience ratings			
Competence Level			

Scoring for APM Levels	
K: 7–10 E: 7–10	Level A: Can successfully execute all the indicators by directing the management of complex projects and/or programmes for an organisation or a functional unit.
K: 6 E: 5–6	Level B: Has successfully executed most of the indicators by managing a complex project.
K: 5 E: 3–4	Level C: Has successfully executed at least some of the indicators by management of a project with limited complexity.
K: 1–4 E: 0–2	Level D: Has the knowledge required and may execute some of the indicators in supporting a project manager and/or project team.

2.14 PROJECT QUALITY MANAGEMENT

Technical competence domain			
TC14	**PROJECT QUALITY MANAGEMENT**		
Definition			
Project quality management is the discipline that is applied to ensure that both the outputs of the project and the processes by which the outputs are delivered meet the required needs of stakeholders. Quality is broadly defined as fitness for purpose or more narrowly as the degree of conformance of the outputs and processes.			
Indicators		**K**	**E**
1	Discusses and agrees the quality expectations and quality criteria with the stakeholders.		
2	Develops a quality approach for the project, including key activities and the application of required quality systems.		
3	Develops the project quality plan, taking into consideration the customer's quality assurance and quality control procedures as appropriate, wherever possible including quantitative criteria against which deliverables can be measured. Agrees the quality plan with the customer.		
4	Executes the project quality plan, carrying out quality assurance and control, and maintains a quality log containing all assurance activities and results.		
5	Recommends and applies continuous improvements and preventative and corrective actions, and reports on impact on quality.		
Total score for knowledge and experience		÷5	÷5
Overall knowledge and experience ratings			
Competence Level			

Scoring for APM Levels	
K: 8–10 E: 7–10	Level A: Can successfully execute all the indicators by directing the management of complex projects and/or programmes for an organisation or a functional unit.
K: 7 E: 6	Level B: Has successfully executed most of the indicators by managing a complex project.
K: 6 E: 4–5	Level C: Has successfully executed at least some of the indicators by management of a project with limited complexity.
K: 5 E: 0–3	Level D: Has the knowledge required and may execute some of the indicators in supporting a project manager and/or project team.

2.15 SCHEDULING

Technical competence domain		K	E
TC15	**SCHEDULING**		
Definition			
Scheduling is the process used to determine the overall project duration and when activities and events are planned to happen. This includes identification of activities and their logical dependencies, and estimation of activity durations, taking into account requirements and availability of resources.			
Indicators		**K**	**E**
Using an appropriate project management planning tool:			
1	Defines and sequences the activities and/or work packages taking into account any dependencies.		
2	Applies estimates of effort and duration considering resource constraints.		
3	Identifies major phases, milestones and appropriate review/gateway points, and schedules the project to determine critical path as appropriate. Considers any points of risk, updating the risk log as appropriate.		
4	Compares target, planned and actual dates, and takes corrective actions or updates forecast as necessary.		
5	Regularly updates the schedule with actuals and estimates to complete and reschedule to determine whether target date and costs remain viable, and checks for any changes to the critical path.		
6	Raises 'out of tolerance' issues and escalates for sponsor decision.		
7	Maintains the schedule with respect to changes.		
Total score for knowledge and experience		÷7	÷7
Overall knowledge and experience ratings			
Competence Level			

Scoring for APM Levels	
K: 8–10 E: 7–10	Level A: Can successfully execute all the indicators by directing the management of complex projects and/or programmes for an organisation or a functional unit.
K: 7 E: 6	Level B: Has successfully executed most of the indicators by managing a complex project.
K: 6 E: 5	Level C: Has successfully executed at least some of the indicators by management of a project with limited complexity.
K: 5 E: 0–4	Level D: Has the knowledge required and may execute some of the indicators in supporting a project manager and/or project team.

2.16 RESOURCE MANAGEMENT

Technical competence domain		K	E
TC16	**RESOURCE MANAGEMENT**		
Definition			
Resource management identifies and assigns resources to activities so that the project is undertaken using appropriate levels of resources and within an acceptable duration. Resource allocation, smoothing, levelling and scheduling are techniques used to determine and manage appropriate levels of resources.			
Indicators		**K**	**E**
1	Identifies what resources are required, including the specific project management effort. The competence required of the personnel in the project team should also be made explicit.		
2	Schedules the resources and applies appropriate smoothing and levelling until an optimised plan is achieved.		
3	Obtains agreement with line management/resource owners for resource assignments to the project.		
4	Places the schedule and resource allocation plan under change control.		
5	Controls the resources with respect to changes to project scope and resource availability.		
6	Manages introduction and release of project resources throughout the project.		
Total score for knowledge and experience		÷6	÷6
Overall knowledge and experience ratings			
Competence Level			

Scoring for APM Levels	
K: 7–10 E: 7–10	Level A: Can successfully execute all the indicators by directing the management of complex projects and/or programmes for an organisation or a functional unit.
K: 6 E: 6	Level B: Has successfully executed most of the indicators by managing a complex project.
K: 5 E: 4–5	Level C: Has successfully executed at least some of the indicators by management of a project with limited complexity.
K: 4 E: 0–3	Level D: Has the knowledge required and may execute some of the indicators in supporting a project manager and/or project team.

2.17 INFORMATION MANAGEMENT AND REPORTING

Technical competence domain			
TC17	**INFORMATION MANAGEMENT AND REPORTING**		
Definition			
Information management is the collection, storage, dissemination, archiving and appropriate destruction of project information. Information reporting takes information and presents it in an appropriate format which includes the formal communication of project information to stakeholders.			
Indicators		**K**	**E**
1	Plans the information management system for the project and agrees it with stakeholders, ensuring all of their information needs are met.		
2	Ensures compliance with the organisation's data and information policies and any regulatory requirements.		
3	Implements the project information management and reporting system.		
4	Implements procedures for processing documents, including incoming and outgoing information, filing and archiving.		
5	Audits the use of the project information management and reporting system.		
6	Communicates the project information to stakeholders.		
Total score for knowledge and experience		÷6	÷6
Overall knowledge and experience ratings			
Competence Level			

Scoring for APM Levels	
K: 7–10 E: 7–10	Level A: Can successfully execute all the indicators by directing the management of complex projects and/or programmes for an organisation or a functional unit.
K: 6 E: 6	Level B: Has successfully executed most of the indicators by managing a complex project.
K: 5 E: 4–5	Level C: Has successfully executed at least some of the indicators by management of a project with limited complexity.
K: 4 E: 0–3	Level D: Has the knowledge required and may execute some of the indicators in supporting a project manager and/or project team.

2.18 PROJECT MANAGEMENT PLAN

Technical competence domain			
TC18	**PROJECT MANAGEMENT PLAN**		
Definition			
The project management plan (PMP) brings together all the plans for a project. The purpose of the PMP is to document the outcomes of the planning process and to provide the reference document for managing the project. The PMP is owned by the project manager.			
Indicators		**K**	**E**
1	Defines the structure and format of the PMP, recognising that it could comprise one or more documents depending on the size, need and complexity of the project.		
2	Works with the project team and stakeholders to ensure that the PMP answers the why, what, how, how much, who, when and where questions for the project.		
3	Documents and confirms the high-level background and rationale for the project, referencing any other relevant detailed documentation (why).		
4	Documents and confirms the overall objectives, scope, high-level deliverables/products (including acceptance criteria) and success criteria (project KPIs) for the project. Ensures constraints, assumptions and dependencies are documented and understood (what).		
5	Documents and confirms the governance for the project, including the life cycle/approach, management controls (reporting and handover mechanisms), relevant tools and techniques (how).		
6	Documents and confirms the project estimates, overall budget and cost management processes (how much).		
7	Documents and confirms the project organisational breakdown structure (OBS), defining key roles and responsibilities, and confirms the resources to be used, including third-party responsibilities (who).		
8	Documents and confirms the project schedule, critical path and key timelines, including milestones (when).		
9	Documents and confirms where the work will be performed, including geographical locations and time zone working arrangements as required for all participants (where).		
10	Obtains formal acceptance of the key elements of the project management plan as they are produced or updated, and places them under configuration management.		
Total score for knowledge and experience		÷10	÷10
Overall knowledge and experience ratings			
Competence Level			

Scoring for APM Levels	
K: 8–10 E: 8–10	Level A: Can successfully execute all the indicators by directing the management of complex projects and/or programmes for an organisation or a functional unit.
K: 7 E: 6–7	Level B: Has successfully executed most of the indicators by managing a complex project.
K: 5–6 E: 4–5	Level C: Has successfully executed at least some of the indicators by management of a project with limited complexity.
K: 1–4 E: 0–3	Level D: Has the knowledge required and may execute some of the indicators in supporting a project manager and/or project team.

2.19 CONFIGURATION MANAGEMENT

Technical competence domain		K	E
TC19	**CONFIGURATION MANAGEMENT**		
Definition			
Configuration management comprises the technical and administrative activities concerned with the creation, maintenance and controlled change of the configuration throughout the project life cycle.			
Indicators		**K**	**E**
1	Prepares and executes a configuration management plan in line with project and organisation requirements.		
2	Identifies, documents and communicates all components of project deliverables and allocates an appropriate configuration numbering system to each which will enable their status and history to be determined.		
3	Identifies the agreed baseline of each deliverable (or deliverable component) and places them under configuration control such that subsequent changes may be made only via the agreed change control procedure.		
4	Documents/records and reports on all current and theoretical data concerned with each configuration item (project deliverables/products).		
5	Carries out reviews and audits to ensure that there is conformity between all configuration items (project deliverables/products).		
Total score for knowledge and experience		÷5	÷5
Overall knowledge and experience ratings			
Competence Level			

Scoring for APM Levels	
K: 8–10 E: 7–10	Level A: Can successfully execute all the indicators by directing the management of complex projects and/or programmes for an organisation or a functional unit.
K: 7 E: 6	Level B: Has successfully executed most of the indicators by managing a complex project.
K: 5–6 E: 4–5	Level C: Has successfully executed at least some of the indicators by management of a project with limited complexity.
K: 4 E: 0–3	Level D: Has the knowledge required and may execute some of the indicators in supporting a project manager and/or project team.

2.20 CHANGE CONTROL

Technical competence domain			
TC20	**CHANGE CONTROL**		
Definition			
Change control is the process that ensures that all changes made to a project's baselined scope, time, cost and quality objectives or agreed benefits are identified, evaluated, approved, rejected or deferred.			
Indicators		**K**	**E**

1	Decides upon, agrees and implements a change management policy for the project that provides a formal mechanism for:
	• recording any issues or proposed changes
	• assessing their likely impact
	• obtaining the relevant stakeholders' decisions on:
	  • rejecting the change
	  • deferring until later
	  • accepting change along with the corresponding changes to cost and timescale.		

2	Captures and logs all proposed changes to the agreed scope and objectives of the project, e.g. a change to accommodate a need not originally defined to be part of the project.		
3	Conducts an impact analysis on the consequences of proposed changes to the project (in terms of time, cost and quality), the business case and benefits management plan.		
4	Defines various responsibilities and authority levels so that routine changes can be dealt with efficiently, but significant changes receive due management attention.		
5	Gets changes accepted or rejected and maintains the change control log.		
6	Plans, executes, controls and closes approved changes.		
7	Reports the status of changes throughout the project.		
Total score for knowledge and experience		÷7	÷7
Overall knowledge and experience ratings			
Competence Level			

Scoring for APM Levels	
K: 8–10 E: 7–10	Level A: Can successfully execute all the indicators by directing the management of complex projects and/or programmes for an organisation or a functional unit.
K: 7 E: 6	Level B: Has successfully executed most of the indicators by managing a complex project.
K: 5–6 E: 4–5	Level C: Has successfully executed at least some of the indicators by management of a project with limited complexity.
K: 4 E: 0–3	Level D: Has the knowledge required and may execute some of the indicators in supporting a project manager and/or project team.

2.21 IMPLEMENTATION

Technical competence domain			
TC21	**IMPLEMENTATION**		
Definition			
Implementation is the third phase of the project life cycle, during which the project management plan is executed, monitored and controlled. In this phase the design is finalised and used to build the deliverables.			
Indicators		**K**	**E**
1	Reviews and revises where necessary the design and build phases of the project management plan.		
2	Executes the design and build phases of the project as defined in the project management plan.		
3	Procures resources, and develops and assigns work packages.		
4	Monitors progress against plan and prepares regular progress reports.		
5	Reviews progress with the sponsor and agrees any remedial actions against project scope and business case, ensuring benefits are still valid.		
6	Assesses risks and maintains the risk log and any mitigation plans.		
7	Assesses issues and ensures follow-up actions are completed.		
8	Manages changes in accordance with the project management plan.		
9	Ensures the quality plan is adhered to and delivers the desired quality of deliverable.		
Total score for knowledge and experience		÷9	÷9
Overall knowledge and experience ratings			
Competence Level			

Scoring for APM Levels	
K: 7–10 E: 7–10	Level A: Can successfully execute all the indicators by directing the management of complex projects and/or programmes for an organisation or a functional unit.
K: 6 E: 5–6	Level B: Has successfully executed most of the indicators by managing a complex project.
K: 5 E: 3–4	Level C: Has successfully executed at least some of the indicators by management of a project with limited complexity.
K: 4 E: 0–2	Level D: Has the knowledge required and may execute some of the indicators in supporting a project manager and/or project team.

2.22 TECHNOLOGY MANAGEMENT

Technical competence domain			
TC22	**TECHNOLOGY MANAGEMENT**		
Definition			
Technology management is the management of the relationship between available and emerging technologies, the organisation and the project. It also includes management of the enabling technologies used to deliver the project, technologies used to manage the project and the technology of the project deliverables.			
Indicators		**K**	**E**
1	Discusses, defines and agrees the technology management strategy for the project, ensuring buy-in from stakeholders and alignment with their overall technology management strategy.		
2	Ensures the risks and opportunities of adopting any new or emerging technologies are fully understood by, communicated to and agreed with relevant stakeholders.		
3	Ensures that the deployment of new technologies is compatible/interfaces with existing technologies and related products, and those which will form the environment into which the project will deliver.		
4	Calculates the cost of the technology management strategy and incorporates corresponding risk premiums into the estimates and resource requirements (skills and competences) for the project.		
5	Monitors the adoption and implementation of the technology management strategy, identifies and escalates issues and risks, and highlights opportunities as soon as these are evident.		
Total score for knowledge and experience		÷5	÷5
Overall knowledge and experience ratings			
Competence Level			

Scoring for APM Levels	
K: 7–10 E: 6–10	Level A: Can successfully execute all the indicators by directing the management of complex projects and/or programmes for an organisation or a functional unit.
K: 5–6 E: 4–5	Level B: Has successfully executed most of the indicators by managing a complex project.
K: 4 E: 3	Level C: Has successfully executed at least some of the indicators by management of a project with limited complexity.
K: 3 E: 0–2	Level D: Has the knowledge required and may execute some of the indicators in supporting a project manager and/or project team.

2.23 BUDGETING AND COST MANAGEMENT

Technical competence domain		K	E
TC23	**BUDGETING AND COST MANAGEMENT**		
Definition			
Budgeting and cost management is the estimating of costs and the setting of an agreed budget, and the management of actual and forecast costs against that budget.			
Indicators		**K**	**E**
1	Estimates and evaluates costs of each work package, including overhead costs using work breakdown structure/product breakdown structure.		
2	Establishes and agrees overall budget, including tolerances, risk premium, assumptions and exclusions based on the business case and investment appraisal.		
3	Identifies when expenditure will take place and develops a cash flow forecast, ensuring funds will be available when required.		
4	Establishes cost monitoring and controlling elements, as well as inflation and currency management if necessary.		
5	Reports on financial performance to stakeholders in line with project and organisation requirements.		
6	Monitors forecast vs. actual resource usage and costs or expenses incurred, taking into account any approved changes.		
7	Captures key project metrics for actuals versus estimates, and ensures these are fed back into the estimating process/systems.		
8	Forecasts cost trends and final costs, noting variations, and develops and applies corrective actions as necessary.		
9	Completes all financial transactions and updates the final costs as per the project and organisation requirements.		
Total score for knowledge and experience		÷9	÷9
Overall knowledge and experience ratings			
Competence Level			

Scoring for APM Levels	
K: 8–10 E: 7–10	Level A: Can successfully execute all the indicators by directing the management of complex projects and/or programmes for an organisation or a functional unit.
K: 7 E: 6	Level B: Has successfully executed most of the indicators by managing a complex project.
K: 6 E: 5	Level C: Has successfully executed at least some of the indicators by management of a project with limited complexity.
K: 5 E: 0–4	Level D: Has the knowledge required and may execute some of the indicators in supporting a project manager and/or project team.

2.24 PROCUREMENT

Technical competence domain		K	E
TC24	**PROCUREMENT**		
Definition			
Procurement is the process by which the resources (goods and services) required by a project are acquired. It includes development of the procurement strategy, preparation of contracts, selection and acquisition of suppliers, and management of the contracts.			
Indicators		**K**	**E**
1	Clarifies requirements and specifications for key products and services.		
2	Investigates the technical and commercial options for fulfilling the requirements, including possible sources of supply, and agrees the preferred options (contractual arrangements) and potential suppliers with the business.		
3	Ensures that suppliers are approved in accordance with company/customer procedures.		
4	Manages the tender, evaluation and selection process.		
5	Negotiates with preferred suppliers, drafts contracts (including appropriate terms and conditions) and technical schedules, and develops acceptance procedures and criteria, recognising the organisation's overarching procurement procedures and authorisation limits as applicable.		
6	Manages the placement of contracts and ensures effective management of the contract in respect of relationship with the suppliers and monitoring of their performance.		
7	Implements, maintains and disseminates procurement strategy, policy, standards, methods and processes relating to the project.		
Total score for knowledge and experience			
		÷7	÷7
Overall knowledge and experience ratings			
Competence Level			

Scoring for APM Levels	
K: 8–10 E: 6–10	Level A: Can successfully execute all the indicators by directing the management of complex projects and/or programmes for an organisation or a functional unit.
K: 7 E: 5	Level B: Has successfully executed most of the indicators by managing a complex project.
K: 5–6 E: 4	Level C: Has successfully executed at least some of the indicators by management of a project with limited complexity.
K: 4 E: 0–3	Level D: Has the knowledge required and may execute some of the indicators in supporting a project manager and/or project team.

2.25 ISSUE MANAGEMENT

Technical competence domain				
TC25	**ISSUE MANAGEMENT**			
Definition				
Issue management is the process by which concerns that threaten the project objectives and cannot be resolved by the project manager are identified and addressed to remove the threats they pose.				
Indicators			**K**	**E**
1	Is aware of the need to manage issues that, if left unresolved, could threaten the success of a project and/or programme.			
2	Prepares and maintains an issue log to facilitate the progress tracking of project/ programme issues from identification to resolution and closure, ensuring each is allocated an owner responsible for resolution.			
3	Is aware of the common failures in the management of issues: • failure to identify the difference between an issue, a problem (a concern that a project manager can deal with on a day-to-day basis) and a risk • failure to escalate to the appropriate level when resolution is not achieved in a timely manner.			
4	Continuously monitors and reports to the project sponsor/project steering group the 'ageing of issues', and ensures that issues are raised with the sponsor/project steering group so that resolution can be reached.			
Total score for knowledge and experience			÷4	÷4
Overall knowledge and experience ratings				
Competence Level				

Scoring for APM Levels	
K: 8–10 E: 7–10	Level A: Can successfully execute all the indicators by directing the management of complex projects and/or programmes for an organisation or a functional unit.
K: 7 E: 6	Level B: Has successfully executed most of the indicators by managing a complex project.
K: 6 E: 4–5	Level C: Has successfully executed at least some of the indicators by management of a project with limited complexity.
K: 5 E: 0–3	Level D: Has the knowledge required and may execute some of the indicators in supporting a project manager and/or project team.

2.26 DEVELOPMENT

Technical competence domain		K	E
TC26	**DEVELOPMENT**		
Definition			
Development is the progressive working up of a preferred solution to an optimised solution during the definition and implementation phases. The optimised solution is refined with the stakeholders against the requirements.			
Indicators		**K**	**E**
1	Identify and agree the development methodology to be used.		
2	Engage with stakeholders and users throughout the development process, managing expectations and maintaining commitment as the solution develops.		
3	Apply a phased development approach with design documentation reviews, quality reviews and lessons-learned reviews as the project proceeds from definition to implementation.		
4	Appreciate and ensure continual management of the solution development through progressive testing of emerging solutions against identified requirements.		
Total score for knowledge and experience		÷4	÷4
Overall knowledge and experience ratings			
Competence Level			

Scoring for APM Levels	
K: 7–10 E: 6–10:	Level A: Can successfully execute all the indicators by directing the management of complex projects and/or programmes for an organisation or a functional unit.
K: 5–6 E: 4–5	Level B: Has successfully executed most of the indicators by managing a complex project.
K: 4 E: 3	Level C: Has successfully executed at least some of the indicators by management of a project with limited complexity.
K: 1–3 E: 0–2	Level D: Has the knowledge required and may execute some of the indicators in supporting a project manager and/or project team.

2.27 VALUE MANAGEMENT

Technical competence domain		K	E
TC27	**VALUE MANAGEMENT**		
Definition			
Value management (VM) is a structured approach to defining what value means to the organisation and the project. It is a framework that allows needs, problems or opportunities to be defined and then enables review of whether the initial project objectives can be improved to determine the optimal approach and solution.			
Indicators		**K**	**E**
1	Understands the concept of value management, the concepts of value and their function and purpose within the project.		
2	Understands the benefits of value management.		
3	Understands the key principles of value management: • management style • positive human dynamics • internal/external environment • methods and tools.		
4	Understands the structure of the VM team and the role of the value manager.		
5	Applies value management when, where and how, as appropriate: • VM interventions and their distinct benefits • initiating a VM study, either as a workshop or continuous application.		
6	Understands and applies VM structured problem solving.		
7	Understands the links between VM and risk management.		
8	Maintains audit trails and records of implementation.		
Total score for knowledge and experience			
		÷8	÷8
Overall knowledge and experience ratings			
Competence Level			

Scoring for APM Levels	
K: 7–10 E: 7–10	Level A: Can successfully execute all the indicators by directing the management of complex projects and/or programmes for an organisation or a functional unit.
K: 5–6 E: 5–6	Level B: Has successfully executed most of the indicators by managing a complex project.
K: 4 E: 3–4	Level C: Has successfully executed at least some of the indicators by management of a project with limited complexity.
K: 1–3 E: 0–2	Level D: Has the knowledge required and may execute some of the indicators in supporting a project manager and/or project team.

2.28 EARNED VALUE MANAGEMENT

Technical competence domain			
TC28	**EARNED VALUE MANAGEMENT**		
Definition			
Earned value management (EVM) is a project control process based on a structured approach to planning, cost collection and performance measurement. It facilitates the integration of project scope and time and cost objectives, and the establishment of a baseline plan for performance measurement.			
Indicators		**K**	**E**
1	Establishes and agrees an integrated and baselined EVM plan by profiling anticipated progress (measured to agreed standard, e.g. delivery, cost, etc.) over time, and places it under configuration control.		
2	Analyses whether the project is ahead or behind the planned schedule.		
3	Continuously measures ongoing efficiency and performance in terms of project scope, time and cost.		
4	Interrogates data to identify problems, corrective actions and replanning if required.		
5	Documents planned work, cost to achieve planned work and whether the work achieved is costing more or less than what was planned.		
6	Where so required by procurement contracts, makes supplier payments according to earned value achievements as agreed.		
7	Calculates, documents and communicates variance and trend analyses through an appropriate change control process.		
Total score for knowledge and experience		÷7	÷7
Overall knowledge and experience ratings			
Competence Level			

Scoring for APM Levels	
K: 8–10 E: 8–10:	Level A: Can successfully execute all the indicators by directing the management of complex projects and/or programmes for an organisation or a functional unit.
K: 6–7 E: 6–7	Level B: Has successfully executed most of the indicators by managing a complex project.
K: 5 E: 4–5	Level C: Has successfully executed at least some of the indicators by management of a project with limited complexity.
K: 1–4 E: 0–3	Level D: Has the knowledge required and may execute some of the indicators in supporting a project manager and/or project team.

2.29 VALUE ENGINEERING

Technical competence domain		K	E
TC29	**VALUE ENGINEERING**		
Definition			
Value engineering (VE) is concerned with optimising the conceptual, technical and operational aspects of a project's deliverables. It utilises a series of proven techniques during the implementation phase of a project.			
Indicators		**K**	**E**
1	Understands the role of value engineering, the concepts of value and their function and purpose, and the link to value management within the project.		
2	Understands the benefits of value engineering.		
3	Knows the key principles of value engineering: • management style • positive human dynamics • internal/external environment • methods and tools.		
4	Understands the structure of the VE team and the role of the value engineer.		
5	Knows when, where and how to apply value engineering.		
6	Has knowledge of VE structured problem solving.		
7	Analyses the structure, scope and context of the project.		
8	Optimises the conceptual, technical and operational aspects of the project.		
9	Understands the links between VE and risk management.		
10	Maintains audit trails and records of implementation, including lessons learned, and applies them to future projects.		
Total score for knowledge and experience		÷10	÷10
Overall knowledge and experience ratings			
Competence Level			

Scoring for APM Levels	
K: 7–10 E: 7–10	Level A: Can successfully execute all the indicators by directing the management of complex projects and/or programmes for an organisation or a functional unit.
K: 5–6 E: 5–6	Level B: Has successfully executed most of the indicators by managing a complex project.
K: 4 E: 3–4	Level C: Has successfully executed at least some of the indicators by management of a project with limited complexity.
K: 1–3 E: 0–2	Level D: Has the knowledge required and may execute some of the indicators in supporting a project manager and/or project team.

2.30 HANDOVER AND CLOSEOUT

Technical competence domain			
TC30	**HANDOVER AND CLOSEOUT**		
Definition			
Handover and closeout is the fourth and final phase in the project life cycle. During this phase final project deliverables are handed over to the sponsor and users. Closeout is the process of finalising all project matters, carrying out final project reviews, archiving project information and redeploying the project team.			
Indicators		**K**	**E**
1	Formalises the project completion process, hands over operational documents and agrees on a process to resolve open issues.		
2	Undertakes an assessment of the readiness of the business to accept and utilise the project deliverables/products.		
3	Ensures that all of the required project deliverables/products have been delivered to and accepted by the required stakeholders, agreeing ownership of any outstanding requests for change and open risks and issues, with plans for resolution.		
4	Obtains appropriate sign-off certificates and agreements on handover of responsibility for all deliverables/products from required stakeholders.		
5	Closes contracts with contractors and suppliers.		
6	Completes all financial transactions and updates the final costs.		
7	Obtains formal project closedown from the project board or other appropriate governance forum.		
8	Evaluates and documents lessons learned, and applies them to future projects.		
9	Releases human resources and other assets, dissolves project organisation, obtains release from project management role and hands over responsibility to project owner.		
10	Archives project records.		
11	Schedules a post-project review to be carried out by the project sponsor at a date in the future.		
Total score for knowledge and experience		$\div 11$	$\div 11$
Overall knowledge and experience ratings			
Competence Level			

Scoring for APM Levels	
K: 8–10 E: 7–10	Level A: Can successfully execute all the indicators by directing the management of complex projects and/or programmes for an organisation or a functional unit.
K: 7 E: 6	Level B: Has successfully executed most of the indicators by managing a complex project.
K: 6 E: 5	Level C: Has successfully executed at least some of the indicators by management of a project with limited complexity.
K: 5 E: 0–4	Level D: Has the knowledge required and may execute some of the indicators in supporting a project manager and/or project team.

THE BEHAVIOURAL COMPETENCE DOMAIN

3

The behavioural competence elements described here encompass the individual behaviours and the people management processes that are essential to the successful delivery of a project (Figure 3.1). The description of each behavioural competence element is designed to be relevant to the profession of project management.

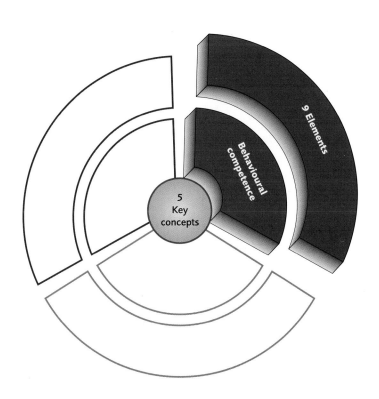

BC01	Communication		**BC06**	Human resource management
BC02	Teamwork		**BC07**	Behavioural characteristics
BC03	Leadership		**BC08**	Learning and development
BC04	Conflict management		**BC09**	Professionalism and ethics
BC05	Negotiation			

Figure 3.1 *The behavioural competence domain*

3.1 COMMUNICATION

Behavioural competence domain		K	E
BC01	**COMMUNICATION**		
Definition			
Communication is the giving, receiving, processing and interpretation of information. Information can be conveyed verbally, non-verbally, actively, passively, formally, informally, consciously or unconsciously.			
Indicators		**K**	**E**
1	Effectively communicates to stakeholders throughout the project's life cycle, enabled by the analysis of stakeholders' and team members' communication needs and preparation of a communication plan.		
2	Develops and executes the communication plan using formal and informal mechanisms as required throughout the project's life cycle and in order to deliver the project successfully.		
3	Acknowledges own personal style of communication and the impacts it has on others (including language, tone and body language). Actively listens and is able to adapt own style appropriate to the situation and target audience.		
4	Seeks feedback on the effectiveness of the communication and continuously revises the plan according to the needs of the audience.		
5	Evaluates and takes appropriate actions on issues that could result in ineffective communication.		
6	Communicates the decisions and the reasons for the decisions to team members. Encourages top-down and bottom-up communication from all members of the project team.		
Total score for knowledge and experience			
		÷6	÷6
Overall knowledge and experience ratings			
Competence Level			

Scoring for APM Levels	
K: 8–10 E: 8–10	Level A: Can successfully execute all the indicators by directing the management of complex projects and/or programmes for an organisation or a functional unit.
K: 7 E: 6–7	Level B: Has successfully executed most of the indicators by managing a complex project.
K: 6 E: 5	Level C: Has successfully executed at least some of the indicators by management of a project with limited complexity.
K: 5 E: 0–4	Level D: Has the knowledge required and may execute some of the indicators in supporting a project manager and/or project team.

3.2 TEAMWORK

Behavioural competence domain			
BC02	**TEAMWORK**		
Definition			
Teamwork is the process whereby people work collaboratively towards a common goal, as distinct from other ways that individuals can work within a group.			
Indicators		**K**	**E**
1	Builds and maintains an effective project team throughout the project life cycle. In doing so is aware of the different stages of team development and the different models that can be applied.		
2	Develops the team objectives and agrees ways of working with the team.		
3	Manages the requirements of the various team members and the circumstances and interests of individuals throughout the project.		
4	Takes pride in the project and the team's achievements, provides regular feedback to the team, and recognises and acknowledges contributions from individual team members.		
5	Communicates regularly with the project team and wider networks.		
6	Asks for support and offers assistance as appropriate.		
7	Contributes positively to address problems and devises solutions with the team.		
Total score for knowledge and experience		÷7	÷7
Overall knowledge and experience ratings			
Competence Level			

Scoring for APM Levels	
K: 8–10 E: 7–10	Level A: Can successfully execute all the indicators by directing the management of complex projects and/or programmes for an organisation or a functional unit.
K: 7 E: 6	Level B: Has successfully executed most of the indicators by managing a complex project.
K: 6 E: 5	Level C: Has successfully executed at least some of the indicators by management of a project with limited complexity.
K: 5 E: 0–4	Level D: Has the knowledge required and may execute some of the indicators in supporting a project manager and/or project team.

3.3 LEADERSHIP

Behavioural competence domain		K	E
BC03	**LEADERSHIP**		
Definition			
Leadership is the ability to establish vision and direction, to influence and align others towards a common purpose, and to empower and inspire people to achieve project success. It enables the project to proceed in an environment of change and uncertainty.			
Indicators		**K**	**E**
1	Promotes and upholds the project vision, reinforces positive relationships, builds an environment that supports effective teamwork, raises morale and empowers and inspires others to follow throughout the life cycle of the project.		
2	Determines what leadership style is appropriate for the particular situation, individual or group, and adapts style as appropriate.		
3	Creates an environment which encourages high performance and enables team members to reach their full potential.		
4	Gains the trust, confidence and commitment of others and utilises collaboration throughout the life cycle to ensure the continued momentum of the project.		
5	Builds and maintains the motivation of the team throughout the project.		
6	Agrees SMART performance objectives for the team and individuals which are regularly reviewed and monitored to provide prompt and constructive feedback.		
7	Identifies and addresses development needs of the team and self.		
Total score for knowledge and experience		÷7	÷7
Overall knowledge and experience ratings			
Competence Level			

Scoring for APM Levels	
K: 7–10 E: 8–10	Level A: Can successfully execute all the indicators by directing the management of complex projects and/or programmes for an organisation or a functional unit.
K: 6 E: 6–7	Level B: Has successfully executed most of the indicators by managing a complex project.
K: 4–5 E: 4–5	Level C: Has successfully executed at least some of the indicators by management of a project with limited complexity.
K: 3 E: 0–3	Level D: Has the knowledge required and may execute some of the indicators in supporting a project manager and/or project team.

3.4 CONFLICT MANAGEMENT

Behavioural competence domain			
BC04	**CONFLICT MANAGEMENT**		
Definition			
Conflict management is the process of identifying and addressing differences that, if unmanaged, would affect project objectives. Effective conflict management prevents differences becoming destructive elements in a project.			
Indicators		**K**	**E**
1	Manages the differences of opinion of stakeholders, recognising the levels of power and influence of each and the potential impact of own views.		
2	Listens to and respects the views and questions of others.		
3	Anticipates and prepares for potential conflict situations that may have an impact on the project.		
4	Identifies when conflict situations arise and ensures that appropriate conflict management techniques are employed to enable effective resolution.		
5	Identifies the root causes rather than the symptoms of the conflict and is creative in seeking paths to resolution.		
6	Implements an agreed solution and monitors the ongoing situation, being alert to signs of emerging conflict.		
7	Knows when to escalate or engage others when conflict cannot be resolved.		
8	Ensures appropriate stakeholders are aware that the conflict has been dealt with to the satisfaction of interested parties and to the benefit of the project.		
Total score for knowledge and experience			
		÷8	÷8
Overall knowledge and experience ratings			
Competence Level			

Scoring for APM Levels	
K: 7–10 E: 8–10	Level A: Can successfully execute all the indicators by directing the management of complex projects and/or programmes for an organisation or a functional unit.
K: 6 E: 7	Level B: Has successfully executed most of the indicators by managing a complex project.
K: 5 E: 5–6	Level C: Has successfully executed at least some of the indicators by management of a project with limited complexity.
K: 4 E: 0–4	Level D: Has the knowledge required and may execute some of the indicators in supporting a project manager and/or project team.

3.5 NEGOTIATION

Behavioural competence domain			
BC05	**NEGOTIATION**		
Definition			
Negotiation is a search for agreement, seeking acceptance, consensus and alignment of views. In a project it can take place on an informal basis throughout the project life cycle or on a formal basis such as during procurement, and between signatories to a contract.			
Indicators		**K**	**E**
1	Identifies areas for negotiation and prioritises appropriately.		
2	Decides on the desired outcome and minimum acceptable position, recognising the extent of own remit and the point at which escalation may become necessary. Distinguishes between negotiating position and real underlying need.		
3	Collects and analyses all available information and develops options to achieve agreement.		
4	Sets out a negotiation strategy, understanding the motivation, wants and needs of all parties.		
5	Ensures the project team and stakeholders fully understand and support the strategy.		
6	Considers practical options and prioritises those presenting the optimal solution for the project.		
7	Negotiates firmly at the content level but maintains a positive personal relationship with all parties involved.		
8	Explores and evaluates responses, repeating steps in the negotiation process as many times as necessary until a satisfactory conclusion is reached.		
9	Ensures the result is documented and communicated to relevant parties.		
Total score for knowledge and experience		÷9	÷9
Overall knowledge and experience ratings			
Competence Level			

Scoring for APM Levels	
K: 7–10 E: 8–10	Level A: Can successfully execute all the indicators by directing the management of complex projects and/or programmes for an organisation or a functional unit.
K: 6 E: 7	Level B: Has successfully executed most of the indicators by managing a complex project.
K: 5 E: 4–6	Level C: Has successfully executed at least some of the indicators by management of a project with limited complexity.
K: 4 E: 0–3	Level D: Has the knowledge required and may execute some of the indicators in supporting a project manager and/or project team.

3.6 HUMAN RESOURCE MANAGEMENT

Behavioural competence domain			
BC06	**HUMAN RESOURCE MANAGEMENT**		
Definition			
Human resource management (HRM) is the understanding and application of the policy and procedures that directly affect the people working within the project team and working group. These policies include recruitment, retention, reward, personal development, training and career development.			
Indicators		**K**	**E**
1	Understands and applies the HRM policies of the organisational units supplying resources to the project and all relevant legal, regulatory and other industry obligations.		
2	Prepares and ensures appropriate induction into the project environment for all project team members.		
3	Explains to each project team member what is expected of them, recognising their individual personal circumstances, motivations, interests and goals, in particular any development opportunities arising from the assignment.		
4	Maintains regular contact with the line managers of team members on issues regarding performance and progress on learning and development opportunities.		
5	On closing down the project, redeploys each team member and releases them to their organisational units, with an appropriate acknowledgement of their contribution to the project.		
Total score for knowledge and experience		÷5	÷5
Overall knowledge and experience ratings			
Competence Level			

Scoring for APM Levels	
K: 6–10 E: 6–10	Level A: Can successfully execute all the indicators by directing the management of complex projects and/or programmes for an organisation or a functional unit.
K: 5 E: 4–5	Level B: Has successfully executed most of the indicators by managing a complex project.
K: 4 E: 3	Level C: Has successfully executed at least some of the indicators by management of a project with limited complexity.
K: 3 E: 0–2	Level D: Has the knowledge required and may execute some of the indicators in supporting a project manager and/or project team.

3.7 BEHAVIOURAL CHARACTERISTICS

Behavioural competence domain			
BC07	**BEHAVIOURAL CHARACTERISTICS**		
Definition			
Behavioural characteristics are the elements that separate and describe a person's preferred way of acting, interacting and reacting in a variety of situations. They complement knowledge and experience and are a function of values, beliefs and identity. They can be used in assessment, engagement and career advice.			
Indicators		**K**	**E**
1	Has an open, positive, 'can-do' attitude which builds confidence and credibility both within the team and stakeholders.		
2	Identifies and adopts sensible, effective, straightforward solutions.		
3	Is open to new ideas, practices and methods and gives consideration to the plurality of the views on the project.		
4	Adapts thinking and behaviour to the requirements of the project, the needs of the sponsor, its environment and the people working on it to ensure a successful outcome.		
5	Articulates innovative strategies and solutions to identify ways of working with disparate resources and interests to achieve project objectives.		
6	Identifies and understands threats and opportunities and takes risks prudently.		
7	Respects all human values and reflects contract particulars, appointment conditions, legal agreements and legislation.		
8	Focuses on project objectives with a strong orientation towards achievement of goals, targets and benefits.		
Total score for knowledge and experience		÷8	÷8
Overall knowledge and experience ratings			
Competence Level			

Scoring for APM Levels	
K: 7–10 E: 7–10	Level A: Can successfully execute all the indicators by directing the management of complex projects and/or programmes for an organisation or a functional unit.
K: 6 E: 6	Level B: Has successfully executed most of the indicators by managing a complex project.
K: 5 E: 4–5	Level C: Has successfully executed at least some of the indicators by management of a project with limited complexity.
K: 3–4 E: 0–3	Level D: Has the knowledge required and may execute some of the indicators in supporting a project manager and/or project team.

3.8 LEARNING AND DEVELOPMENT

Behavioural competence domain			
BC08	**LEARNING AND DEVELOPMENT**		
Definition			
Learning and development involves the continual improvement of competencies in the organisation. The identification and application of learning within projects develops the organisation's capability to undertake current and future projects.			
Indicators		**K**	**E**
1	Develops the team and self according to the learning and development policies and processes of the organisation.		
2	Assesses the skills and levels of competence of project team members and identifies any development needs.		
3	Assists and identifies development opportunities, and encourages project team members to undertake learning and development.		
4	Evaluates the extent to which team members have applied the knowledge and skills gained during their development.		
5	Considers learning and development to be a lifelong activity, and is aware of and promotes the need to undertake continuing professional development (CPD) in order to keep pace with changing standards, techniques and methods.		
Total score for knowledge and experience		÷5	÷5
Overall knowledge and experience ratings			
Competence Level			

Scoring for APM Levels	
K: 7–10 E: 6–10	Level A: Can successfully execute all the indicators by directing the management of complex projects and/or programmes for an organisation or a functional unit.
K: 5–6 E: 5	Level B: Has successfully executed most of the indicators by managing a complex project.
K: 4 E: 2–4	Level C: Has successfully executed at least some of the indicators by management of a project with limited complexity.
K: 1–3 E: 0–1	Level D: Has the knowledge required and may execute some of the indicators in supporting a project manager and/or project team.

3.9 PROFESSIONALISM AND ETHICS

Behavioural competence domain			
BC09	PROFESSIONALISM AND ETHICS		
Definition			
Professionalism and ethics both relate to proper conduct. Professionalism is demonstrable awareness and application of qualities and competences covering knowledge, appropriate skills and behaviours. Ethics covers the conduct and moral principles recognised as appropriate within the project management profession.			
Indicators		K	E
1	Honestly represents self at the appropriate level of competence which can be evidenced by appropriate continuing professional development, qualifications, knowledge and experience.		
2	Understands the commercial and legal aspects of the relationship between the client and project manager, and behaves with integrity and in an equitable manner with good faith and good conscience.		
3	Adopts a morally, legally and socially appropriate manner of behaviour and working with all members of the project team and stakeholders.		
4	Is alert to possible unethical situations arising, or proposals being made, that affect the project, the environment and individuals working on it. Is sure to maintain transparency in bringing such issues into the open and escalating them to resolve differences.		
5	Encourages a culture of openness and honesty within the project.		
Total score for knowledge and experience		÷5	÷5
Overall knowledge and experience ratings			
Competence Level			

Scoring for APM Levels	
K: 7–10 E: 7–10	Level A: Can successfully execute all the indicators by directing the management of complex projects and/or programmes for an organisation or a functional unit.
K: 6 E: 6	Level B: Has successfully executed most of the indicators by managing a complex project.
K: 5 E: 4–5	Level C: Has successfully executed at least some of the indicators by management of a project with limited complexity.
K: 4 E: 0–3	Level D: Has the knowledge required and may execute some of the indicators in supporting a project manager and/or project team.

4

THE CONTEXTUAL COMPETENCE DOMAIN

The contextual competence elements describe the concepts of project, programme and portfolio, and the linkage between these concepts and the organisation or organisations that are involved in the project (Figure 4.1).

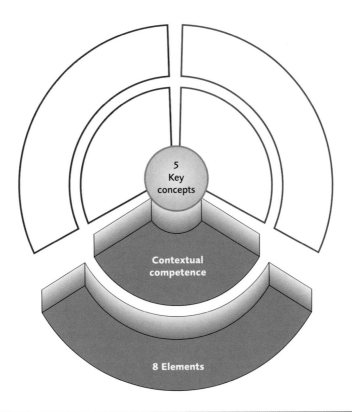

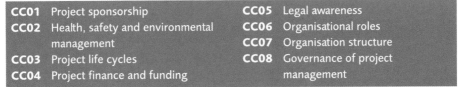

CC01	Project sponsorship	**CC05**	Legal awareness
CC02	Health, safety and environmental management	**CC06**	Organisational roles
		CC07	Organisation structure
CC03	Project life cycles	**CC08**	Governance of project management
CC04	Project finance and funding		

Figure 4.1 *The contextual competence domain*

4.1 PROJECT SPONSORSHIP

Contextual competence domain			
CC01	**PROJECT SPONSORSHIP**		
Definition			
Project sponsorship is an active senior management role, responsible for identifying the business need, problem or opportunity. The sponsor ensures that the project remains a viable proposition and that benefits are realised, resolving any issues outside the control of the project manager.			
Indicators		**K**	**E**
1	Is aware of what motivates the various stakeholders and is able and empowered to address their interest in the project.		
2	Is aware of the role and responsibilities of the project sponsor (executive) and how it changes through the project life cycle.		
3	Is aware of the levels of commitment and support needed for effective project sponsorship.		
4	Demonstrates why effective sponsorship is important to project management, having the following key attributes for a sponsor: • is a business leader and decision-maker across functional boundaries • is an advocate for change and the project • is committed in terms of time and support required of the role • is experienced in project management.		
5	Ensures that any obstacles faced by a project are addressed.		
Total score for knowledge and experience		÷5	÷5
Overall knowledge and experience ratings			
Competence Level			

Scoring for APM Levels	
K: 8–10 E: 7–10	Level A: Can successfully execute all the indicators by directing the management of complex projects and/or programmes for an organisation or a functional unit.
K: 7 E: 5–6	Level B: Has successfully executed most of the indicators by managing a complex project.
K: 5–6 E: 4	Level C: Has successfully executed at least some of the indicators by management of a project with limited complexity.
K: 3–4 E: 0–3	Level D: Has the knowledge required and may execute some of the indicators in supporting a project manager and/or project team.

4.2 HEALTH, SAFETY AND ENVIRONMENTAL MANAGEMENT

Contextual competence domain			
CC02	**HEALTH, SAFETY AND ENVIRONMENTAL MANAGEMENT**		
Definition			
Health, safety and environmental management is the process of determining and applying appropriate standards and methods to minimise the likelihood of accidents, injuries or environmental impact both during the project and during the operation of its deliverables.			
Indicators		**K**	**E**
1	Applies appropriate laws and regulations.		
2	Identifies health, safety and environmental risk and impact of the project.		
3	Develops plans and implements processes to manage the impact on health, safety and the environment.		
4	Monitors and controls the effectiveness of the plans.		
5	Reports health, safety and environmental issues and risks.		
6	Documents lessons learned and applies them to future projects, to phases of the project or elsewhere in the organisation.		
Total score for knowledge and experience		÷6	÷6
Overall knowledge and experience ratings			
Competence Level			

Scoring for APM Levels	
K: 6–10 E: 6–10	Level A: Can successfully execute all the indicators by directing the management of complex projects and/or programmes for an organisation or a functional unit.
K: 5 E: 5	Level B: Has successfully executed most of the indicators by managing a complex project.
K: 4 E: 3–4	Level C: Has successfully executed at least some of the indicators by management of a project with limited complexity.
K: 3 E: 0–2	Level D: Has the knowledge required and may execute some of the indicators in supporting a project manager and/or project team.

4.3 PROJECT LIFE CYCLES

Contextual competence domain			
CC03	**PROJECT LIFE CYCLES**		
Definition			
Project life cycles consist of a number of distinct phases. All projects follow a life cycle, and life cycles will differ across industries and business sectors. A life cycle allows the project to be considered as a sequence of phases which provides the structure and approach for progressively delivering the required outputs.			
Indicators		**K**	**E**
1	Identifies an appropriate life cycle model for the project, taking into account the project characteristics and environment.		
2	Phases the project accordingly, with a suitable number of evaluation and approval points (gates) to monitor project progress.		
3	Uses the project phases for effective cost management of resources.		
Total score for knowledge and experience		÷3	÷3
Overall knowledge and experience ratings			
Competence Level			

Scoring for APM Levels	
K: 7–10 E: 7–10	Level A: Can successfully execute all the indicators by directing the management of complex projects and/or programmes for an organisation or a functional unit.
K: 6 E: 6	Level B: Has successfully executed most of the indicators by managing a complex project.
K: 5 E: 4–5	Level C: Has successfully executed at least some of the indicators by management of a project with limited complexity.
K: 4 E: 0–3	Level D: Has the knowledge required and may execute some of the indicators in supporting a project manager and/or project team.

4.4 PROJECT FINANCE AND FUNDING

Contextual competence domain			
CC04	**PROJECT FINANCE AND FUNDING**		
Definition			
Project financing and funding is the means by which the capital to undertake a project is initially secured and then made available at the appropriate time. Projects may be financed externally or funded internally, or there may be a combination of both.			
Indicators		**K**	**E**
1	Analyses financing options/models for project or programme, including private finance initiatives, public–private partnership, etc.		
2	Negotiates with possible sources of funds and determines conditions attached.		
3	Selects and secures an appropriate source of project funding, with the approval of the project sponsor and/or organisation.		
4	Calculates financial resource usage and cash flows of the project or programme.		
5	Establishes and controls processes and authorisations for payments.		
6	Recognises or establishes and controls bookkeeping and financial auditing systems.		
7	Validates and manages budgets, covering actual costs incurred to date and forecasts to complete, and reports as required to the project sponsor and the organisation.		
Total score for knowledge and experience		÷7	÷7
Overall knowledge and experience ratings			
Competence Level			

Scoring for APM Levels	
K: 6–10 E: 6–10	Level A: Can successfully execute all the indicators by directing the management of complex projects and/or programmes for an organisation or a functional unit.
K: 5 E: 5	Level B: Has successfully executed most of the indicators by managing a complex project.
K: 4 E: 3–4	Level C: Has successfully executed at least some of the indicators by management of a project with limited complexity.
K: 3 E: 0–2	Level D: Has the knowledge required and may execute some of the indicators in supporting a project manager and/or project team.

4.5 LEGAL AWARENESS

Contextual competence domain			
CC05	**LEGAL AWARENESS**		
Definition			
Legal awareness provides project management professionals with an understanding of the relevant legal duties, rights and processes that should be applied to projects.			
Indicators		**K**	**E**
1	Is aware of and applies the legal and contractual requirements within which the project/programme operates, being aware of own commercial obligations and personal liability.		
2	Investigates and describes for the organisation or portfolio the relevant legal aspects that apply to the project.		
3	Initiates and manages processes to ensure that any legal or contractual requirements are adhered to, covering: • time • payments • performance indicators • termination • claims and disputes.		
4	Responds appropriately to claims of harassment, discrimination, safety issues or non-performance.		
Total score for knowledge and experience			
		÷4	÷4
Overall knowledge and experience ratings			
Competence Level			

Scoring for APM Levels	
K: 6–10 E: 6–10	Level A: Can successfully execute all the indicators by directing the management of complex projects and/or programmes for an organisation or a functional unit.
K: 5 E: 4–5	Level B: Has successfully executed most of the indicators by managing a complex project.
K: 4 E: 3	Level C: Has successfully executed at least some of the indicators by management of a project with limited complexity.
K: 3 E: 0–2	Level D: Has the knowledge required and may execute some of the indicators in supporting a project manager and/or project team.

4.6 ORGANISATIONAL ROLES

Contextual competence domain			
CC06	**ORGANISATIONAL ROLES**		
Definition			
Organisational roles are the roles performed by individuals or groups in a project. Both roles and responsibilities within projects must be defined to address the transient and unique nature of projects and to ensure that clear accountabilities can be assigned.			
Indicators		**K**	**E**
1	Defines an appropriate organisation for the management of the project (organisational breakdown structure, OBS), taking into consideration the context, complexity and business impact of the project.		
2	Defines roles, responsibilities, interfaces, levels of authority and procedures in the project, taking account of the transient and unique nature of projects, in accordance with the OBS for the project, and agrees with and appoints the necessary person(s) to these roles.		
3	Ensures that the accountability and responsibilities of the roles are clearly understood by the project team and stakeholders.		
4	Maintains, updates and changes the project organisation during the project life cycle if needed.		
Total score for knowledge and experience		÷4	÷4
Overall knowledge and experience ratings			
Competence Level			

Scoring for APM Levels	
K: 7–10 E: 6–10	Level A: Can successfully execute all the indicators by directing the management of complex projects and/or programmes for an organisation or a functional unit.
K: 6 E: 4–5	Level B: Has successfully executed most of the indicators by managing a complex project.
K: 5 E: 3	Level C: Has successfully executed at least some of the indicators by management of a project with limited complexity.
K: 4 E: 0–2	Level D: Has the knowledge required and may execute some of the indicators in supporting a project manager and/or project team.

4.7 ORGANISATION STRUCTURE

Contextual competence domain			
CC07	**ORGANISATION STRUCTURE**		
Definition			
The organisation structure is the organisational environment within which the project takes place. The organisation structure defines the reporting and decision-making hierarchy of an organisation and how project management operates within it.			
Indicators		**K**	**E**
1	Understands the varying organisational structures (functional, matrix and project, etc.) employed by different organisations, and knows which structures operate across the project's environment.		
2	Identifies all the organisational units that will provide resources to the project.		
3	Uses the project organisational breakdown structure (OBS) and defines roles and responsibilities to develop the interfaces between the project and the different parts of the organisation.		
4	Agrees mechanisms to obtain resources from the organisational units.		
5	Maintains, and updates when required, the interfaces with the units of the permanent organisation.		
6	Determines the requirement for a project office and agrees its remit, levels of authority and position within the organisation.		
Total score for knowledge and experience		÷6	÷6
Overall knowledge and experience ratings			
Competence Level			

Scoring for APM Levels	
K: 8–10 E: 8–10	Level A: Can successfully execute all the indicators by directing the management of complex projects and/or programmes for an organisation or a functional unit.
K: 7 E: 6–7	Level B: Has successfully executed most of the indicators by managing a complex project.
K: 6 E: 4–5	Level C: Has successfully executed at least some of the indicators by management of a project with limited complexity.
K: 5 E: 0–3	Level D: Has the knowledge required and may execute some of the indicators in supporting a project manager and/or project team.

4.8 GOVERNANCE OF PROJECT MANAGEMENT

Contextual competence domain		K	E
CC08	**GOVERNANCE OF PROJECT MANAGEMENT**		
Definition			
Governance of project management (GoPM) concerns those areas of corporate governance that are specifically related to project activities. Effective governance of project management ensures that an organisation's project portfolio is aligned to the organisation's objectives, is delivered efficiently and is sustainable.			
Indicators		**K**	**E**
1	Applies the organisation's overarching governance structure, ensuring that it is understood and that the points of interface with the project are clear and workable.		
2	Applies the relevant organisation processes, standards and guidelines, ensuring that they are taken into account in the project plans, and that appropriate key points in the project (as a minimum, initiation, review gates, handover and close) are communicated to the wider community.		
Total score for knowledge and experience		÷2	÷2
Overall knowledge and experience ratings			
Competence Level			

Scoring for APM Levels	
K: 7–10 E: 8–10	Level A: Can successfully execute all the indicators by directing the management of complex projects and/or programmes for an organisation or a functional unit.
K: 6 E: 6–7	Level B: Has successfully executed most of the indicators by managing a complex project.
K: 5 E: 4–5	Level C: Has successfully executed at least some of the indicators by management of a project with limited complexity.
K: 1–4 E: 0–3	Level D: Has the knowledge required and may execute some of the indicators in supporting a project manager and/or project team.

APPENDICES

SELF-ASSESSMENT SUMMARY SHEET

NAME:						DATE:		
Technical competence elements			**Behavioural competence elements**			**Contextual competence elements**		
Code	Name	Rating	Code	Name	Rating	Code	Name	Rating
TC01	Concept		BC01	Communication		CC01	Project sponsorship	
TC02	Project success and benefits management		BC02	Teamwork		CC02	Health, safety and environmental management	
TC03	Stakeholder management		BC03	Leadership		CC03	Project life cycles	
TC04	Requirements management		BC04	Conflict management		CC04	Project finance and funding	
TC05	Project risk management		BC05	Negotiation		CC05	Legal awareness	
TC06	Estimating		BC06	Human resource management		CC06	Organisational roles	
TC07	Business case		BC07	Behavioural characteristics		CC07	Organisation structure	
TC08	Marketing and sales		BC08	Learning and development		CC08	Governance of project management	
TC09	Project reviews		BC09	Professionalism and ethics				
TC10	Definition							
TC11	Scope management							
TC12	Modelling and testing							
TC13	Methods and procedures							
TC14	Project quality management							
TC15	Scheduling							
TC16	Resource management							
TC17	Information management and reporting							
TC18	Project management plan							
TC19	Configuration management							
TC20	Change control							
TC21	Implementation							
TC22	Technology management							
TC23	Budgeting and cost management							
TC24	Procurement							
TC25	Issue management							
TC26	Development							
TC27	Value management							
TC28	Earned value management							
TC29	Value engineering							
TC30	Handover and closeout							

Personal notes:

For Reference:

Level A: Can successfully execute all the indicators by directing the management of complex projects and/or programmes for an organisation or a functional unit.

Level B: Has successfully executed most of the indicators by managing a complex project.

Level C: Has successfully executed at least some of the indicators by management of a project with limited complexity.

Level D: Has the knowledge required and may execute some of the indicators in supporting a project manager and/or project team.

TC: technical competence; **BC:** behavioural competence; **CC:** contextual competence.

ADAPTING THE *APM COMPETENCE FRAMEWORK*

The *APM Competence Framework* was designed to be comprehensive, meeting the needs of a very broad range of individual and organisational circumstances. Consequently, in any given situation there will be some elements which are more relevant than others, and the following paragraphs are designed to provide guidance, both to individuals and organisations, on how best to undertake any necessary tailoring.

INDIVIDUALS

There are a number of reasons why you might wish to tailor the framework. One might be simply the time you have available for the assessment exercise; other examples are given below. Please note, however, that if you intend to assess your readiness to undertake an examination for an APM professional qualification, you are required to assess yourself using the complete unmodified framework.

The options available to you when tailoring the framework are to modify the scope of the assessment or to modify the depth of the assessment, or both. You need to remember, though, that what you get out of the exercise will depend on what you put in – so avoid over-modification.

Modifying the scope

There are circumstances in which there may be limited value in assessing yourself against some of the elements. Here are two such cases:

- You wish to identify your personal training and developmental needs. Your organisation already requires you to assess yourself against its own competence framework which has elements that overlap with or duplicate elements in the *APM Competence Framework*. In this instance, you may choose to omit from your assessment those competence elements that are catered for elsewhere.
- You wish to confirm that you have the right Level of Competence across a range of skills to apply for a particular post. The role calls for only a subset of the project management competences. You may decide, in this instance, to assess yourself against these alone.

Modifying the depth

The framework is designed to enable an individual to build up an assessment of their Competence Level for each competence element by scoring their knowledge and experience against a number of indicators. The Level of Competence for that competence element is calculated on the basis of an average of these scores. This process helps to ensure that the right factors are taken into consideration and also helps to reduce subjectivity. However, if you wish, you can assess yourself simply at the competence element level, reading through the list of indicators and then inputting an overall score for the competence element as a whole.

Such a modification of the assessment process obviously makes it quicker and easier to do, but it is also more susceptible to bias. If you have the time, you are encouraged to undertake the full assessment. There may be instances when it would be appropriate to fully assess some competence elements and use the quicker method for others.

Modifying both scope and depth

In some circumstances it may be appropriate to make some modification to both the scope and the depth. When deciding whether and how to modify the framework, you will need to consider which competences are most relevant to the organisation and to your current role, or a role to which you aspire. Your line manager or HR department may be able to provide further guidance.

ORGANISATIONS

Every organisation will have its own perspective on competence and its own set of requirements with respect to a competence framework. However, those organisations for which project management is the predominant profession should have no difficulty in adopting the whole framework as a means of assessing their project managers and helping them develop their competence, particularly if they allow individuals some freedom to tailor the scope and/or depth as suggested above.

Many organisations employ staff in a number of professions and, consequently, may have had to take account of a number of existing competence frameworks relating to those professions. In such cases, adding the *APM Competence Framework* should be relatively straightforward. Some larger organisations, however, will have developed their own comprehensive competence framework(s), incorporating elements from a number of professional bodies. In such cases, the APM believes that the flexibility of its framework allows it to be adapted and tailored to provide the project management component of most existing competence frameworks. Where these already exist, they will probably be sector-specific, if not organisationally specific. If the organisation is looking to develop and maintain a level of project management professionalism recognised across industry and government, it will wish to be assured that its competence framework takes account of best practice and appropriately incorporates the *APM Competence Framework*.

The options for tailoring the *APM Competence Framework* to enable it to be integrated with any existing framework(s) include those available to the individual identified above, i.e. modifying scope and depth, but also include modifying the scoring method.

Modifying the scope

Where there is a need to tailor the *APM Competence Framework* so that a subset of it forms part of an existing framework, the APM recommends that the process starts with an examination of the competence elements contained in the technical domain. This is because these tend to be focused on techniques that are primarily, sometimes exclusively, used by project managers and, therefore, most appropriately defined by the project management profession.

In the subsequent review of the behavioural and contextual domains, it is more likely that the constituent competences will already be catered for in some form within the organisation's existing framework and will be multidisciplinary in nature. The important question in these cases will revolve around which is most fit for purpose. In most cases, even if it is not appropriate to use the APM competence element unamended, it should be possible to 'align' an organisation's competences to those in the *APM Competence Framework*. Any significant non-alignment should be examined closely, as it may indicate a gap in the organisation's framework, or an element that is not appropriate to project management.

Modifying the depth

Having identified the scope of the *APM Competence Framework* to be adopted, the organisation could allow its project managers to determine whether to use the full assessment process or the quicker process set out in the 'Individuals' section under 'Modifying the depth' above. Alternatively, this decision could be delegated to line managers, or it could be determined by the organisation as a matter of policy.

Modifying the scoring method

The APM recognises that there is real value in assessing knowledge and experience separately, and then determining a Competence Level taking account of both. For each competence element a table is provided to enable the translation of average indicator scores into an overall Competence Level, which aligns to the levels set down by the International Project Management Association. However, organisations may wish to use a different set of levels (e.g. 1–10, A–D, or Awareness, Practitioner, Expert, etc.) depending upon what existing scoring methods are used.

Further guidance on adapting the framework for organisations can be obtained from the APM.

PROJECT COMPLEXITY MATRIX

Identification of Certification Cycle	This scheme is used to assess the complexity of project management in a project. Each indicator is rated according to four levels of complexity (4 = very high complexity, 3 = high complexity, 2 = low complexity, 1 = very low complexity). If the total complexity value equals or exceeds 25 points, a project is appropriate to be used in a certification process on APM Level B.
Candidate (Last name, first name)	Ratings between 23 and 27 points need careful verification. For a complete evaluation all criteria must be rated.

Criteria	Description of criteria				Value	Comments/justification
	Significant complexity		Limited complexity			
	complexity very high (4)	complexity high (3)	complexity low (2)	complexity very low (1)		
1. Objectives, Assessment of Results						
Mandate and objective	uncertain, vague ←			→ defined, obvious		2/3
Conflicting objectives	many conflicts ←			→ few conflicts		
Transparency of mandate and objectives	hidden ←			→ quite transparent		
Interdependence of objectives	very interdependent ←			→ quite independent		
Number and assessment of results	large, multidimensional ←			→ low, unidimensional		
Rating	☐	☐	☐	☐		
2. Interested Parties, Integration						
Interested parties, lobbies	numerous parties ←			→ few parties		3
Categories of stakeholders	many different ←			→ few uniform categories		
Stakeholder interrelations	unknown relations ←		→ few and well-known relations			
Interests of involved parties	divergent interests ←			→ comparable interest		
Rating	☐	☐	☐	☐		
3. Cultural and Social Context						
Diversity of context	diverse ←			→ homogeneous		2
Cultural variety	multicultural, unknown ←			→ uniform, well known		
Geographic distances	distant, distributed ←			→ close, concentrated		
Social span	large, demanding ←			→ small, easy to handle		
Rating	☐	☐	☐	☐		
4. Degree of Innovation, General Conditions						
Technological degree of innovation	unknown technology ←		→ known and proven technology			2
Demand of creativity	innovative approach ←			→ repetitive approach		
Scope for development	large ←			→ limited		
Significance on public agenda	large public interest ←			→ public interest low		
Rating	☐	☐	☐	☐		
5. Project Structure, Demand for Coordination						
Structures to be coordinated	numerous structures ←			→ few structures		2.5
Demand of coordination	demanding, elaborate ←			→ simple, straightforward		
Structuring of phases	overlapping, simultaneous ←			→ sequential		
Demand for reporting	multidimensional, comprehensive ←			→ unidimensional, common		
Rating	☐	☐	☐	☐		
6. Project Organisation						
Number of interfaces	many ←			→ few		3
Demand for communication	indirect, demanding, manifold ←		→ direct, not demanding, uniform			
Hierarchical structure	multidimensional, matrix structure ←			→ unidimensional, simple		
Relations with permanent organisations	intensive mutual relations ←			→ few relations		
Rating	☐	☐	☐	☐		
7. Leadership, Teamwork, Decisions						
Number of subordinates	many, large control span ←			→ few, small control span		2
Team structure	dynamic team structure ←			→ static team structure		
Leadership style	adaptive and variable ←			→ constant and uniform		
Decision-making processes	many important decisions ←			→ few important decisions		
Rating	☐	☐	☐	☐		
8. Resources, incl. Finance						
Availability of people, material, etc.	uncertain, changing ←			→ available, known		2.5
Financial resources	many investors and kinds of resources ←		→ one investor and few kinds of resources			
Capital investment	large (relative to project of the same kind) ←		→ low (relative to project of the same kind)			
Quantity and diversity of staff	high ←			→ low		
Rating	☐	☐	☐	☐		
9. Risks and Opportunities						
Predictability of risks and opportunities	low, uncertain ←			→ high, quite certain		2
Risk probability, significance of impacts	high risk potential, large impact ←			→ low risk potential, low impact		
Options for actions to minimise risks	limited options for actions ←			→ many options for actions		
Potential of opportunities	large potential of opportunities ←			→ low potential of opportunities		
Rating	☐	☐	☐	☐		
10. PM Methods, Tools and Techniques						
Variety of methods and tools applied	numerous, manifold ←			→ few, simple		2
Application of standards	few common standards applicable ←			→ common standards applicable		
Availability of support	no support available ←			→ much support available		
Proportion of PM to total project work	high percentage ←			→ low percentage		
Rating						
Total complexity value						23

81

THE *APM COMPETENCE FRAMEWORK* AND ITS RELATIONSHIP WITH THE *APM BODY OF KNOWLEDGE* AND *ICB-IPMA COMPETENCE BASELINE*

THE LINK BETWEEN THE *APM BODY OF KNOWLEDGE* AND THE *APM COMPETENCE FRAMEWORK*

The Association for Project Management has set out the principles that define project management in its publication of the *APM Body of Knowledge* (5th edn). It considers the knowledge essential to its practice as part of the establishment of the project management profession and aims to provide the initial knowledge base for project managers, rather than the processes and practices of project management. Table A4.1 overleaf shows how the *APM Body of Knowledge* is divided into seven sections covering 52 knowledge areas.

The *APM Body of Knowledge* describes in very clear terms what project management is, but it does not define the skills or levels of skill required of those who practise project management as a profession. This is the purpose of the *APM Competence Framework*, which has been designed to complement the *APM Body of Knowledge*, and which sets out what project managers need to be able to do well to become effective project managers.

Table A4.1 *Overview of the* APM Body of Knowledge *(5th edn)*

General	
Project management in context	
1.1 Project management	
1.2 Programme management	
1.3 Portfolio management	
1.4 Project context	
1.5 Project sponsorship	
1.6 Project office	

Strategic	
Planning the strategy	**Business and commercial**
2.1 Project success and benefits management	5.1 Business case
2.2 Stakeholder management	5.2 Marketing and sales
2.3 Value management	5.3 Project financing and funding
2.4 Project management plan	5.4 Procurement
2.5 Project risk management	5.5 Legal awareness
2.6 Project quality management	
2.7 Health, safety and environmental management	
Executing the strategy	**Organisation and governance**
3.1 Scope management	6.1 Project life cycles
3.2 Scheduling	6.2 Concept
3.3 Resource management	6.3 Definition
3.4 Budgeting and cost management	6.4 Implementation
3.5 Change control	6.5 Handover and closeout
3.6 Earned value management	6.6 Project reviews
3.7 Information management and reporting	6.7 Organisation structure
3.8 Issue management	6.8 Organisational roles
	6.9 Methods and procedures
	6.10 Governance of project management
Techniques	**People and the profession**
4.1 Requirements management	7.1 Communication
4.2 Development	7.2 Teamwork
4.3 Estimating	7.3 Leadership
4.4 Technology management	7.4 Conflict management
4.5 Value engineering	7.5 Negotiation
4.6 Modelling and testing	7.6 Human resource management
4.7 Configuration management	7.7 Behavioural characteristics
	7.8 Learning and development
	7.9 Professionalism and ethics

THE LINK BETWEEN THE *ICB-IPMA COMPETENCE BASELINE* AND THE *APM COMPETENCE FRAMEWORK*

The Association for Project Management is a member of IPMA, the international network of national project management associations of the project management community and project management profession. The APM's linkage to the IPMA aims to ensure a seamless community of project management that has its standards and processes clearly defined, which allows for the transfer and measurement of knowledge and experience in the international sphere.

The *ICB-IPMA Competence Baseline* (ICB) provides a definition of the competences expected from project management personnel by IPMA certification, using the universal IPMA four-level certification system which the APM applies to its qualification programme.

The ICB comprises 46 competence elements that the IPMA uses as the basis for certification by the international bodies of its member associations, as shown in Figure A4.1.

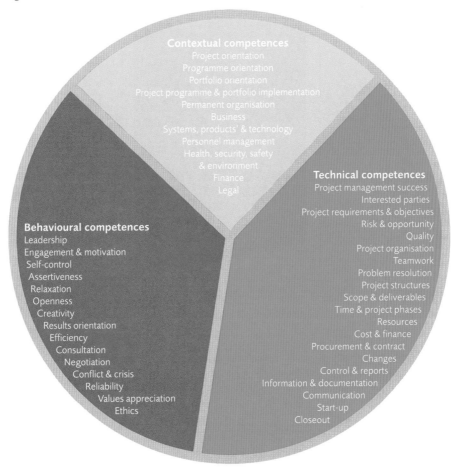

Figure A4.1 *IPMA competence elements*

THE ICB AND APM COMPETENCE TABLES

The *APM Competence Framework* addresses the UK's preference for competence elements, and expresses national cultural differences from the international baseline by adding the specific elements and content linked to the *APM Body of Knowledge*. The *APM Competence Framework* is directly linked to the ICB standard as shown in Figure A5.1.

IPMA Competences legend:

1.01 Project management success · 1.02 Interested parties · 1.03 Project requirements and objectives · 1.04 Risk and opportunity · 1.05 Quality · 1.06 Project organisation · 1.07 Teamwork · 1.08 Problem resolution · 1.09 Project structures · 1.10 Scope and deliverables · 1.11 Time and project phases · 1.12 Resources · 1.13 Cost and finance · 1.14 Procurement and contract · 1.15 Changes · 1.16 Control and reports · 1.17 Information and documentation · 1.18 Communication · 1.19 Start-up · 1.20 Closeout · 2.01 Leadership · 2.02 Engagement and motivation · 2.03 Self-control · 2.04 Assertiveness · 2.05 Relaxation · 2.06 Openness · 2.07 Creativity · 2.08 Results orientation · 2.09 Efficiency · 2.10 Consultation · 2.11 Negotiation · 2.12 Conflict and crisis · 2.13 Reliability · 2.14 Values appreciation · 2.15 Ethics · 3.01 Project orientation · 3.02 Programme orientation · 3.03 Portfolio orientation · 3.04 PPP implementation · 3.05 Permanent organisation · 3.06 Business · 3.07 Systems, products and technology · 3.08 Personnel management · 3.09 Health, security, safety and environment · 3.10 Finance · 3.11 Legal

APM Competences — APM Competence Framework elements (with IPMA Competence mappings):

APM BoK topic	Code	Element	IPMA Competences (marked)
1.1	KC01	Project management	3.01
1.2	KC02	Programme management	3.02
1.3	KC03	Portfolio management	3.03
1.4	KC04	Project context	3.01, 3.04
1.6	KC05	Project office	
6.2	TC01	Concept	1.19
2.1	TC02	Project success & benefits management	1.01
2.2	TC03	Stakeholder management	1.02
4.1	TC04	Requirements management	1.03
2.5	TC05	Project risk management	1.04
4.3	TC06	Estimating	
5.1	TC07	Business case	
5.2	TC08	Marketing & sales	
6.6	TC09	Project reviews	
6.3	TC10	Definition	
3.1	TC11	Scope management	1.10
4.6	TC12	Modelling & testing	
6.9	TC13	Methods & procedures	
2.6	TC14	Project quality management	1.05

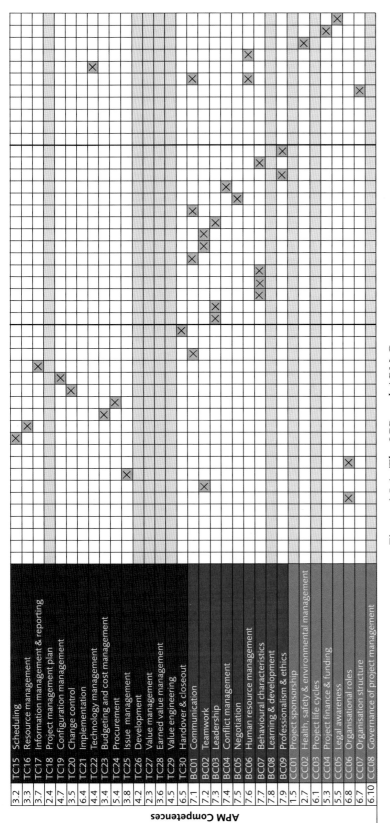

Figure A5.1 *The ICB and APM Competences*

Highlighted are the APM Competences appearing only in the *APM Body of Knowledge* (5th edition)

☒ represents the principal correlation between APM and IPMA Competences

APM TAXONOMY

Tables A6.1, A6.2 and A6.3 show the scoring for knowledge and experience required for APM Level D to Level A against each competence within the *APM Competence Framework*.

Each project management competence element is composed of knowledge and experience. The total competence required per domain should be split between the domains in the proportions shown in Table A6.4.

The knowledge and experience requirements vary according to level as well: the values in Table A6.5 represent the average scores expected of a candidate at each APM Level. The value of competence is graded along a scale from 0 to 10 for knowledge as well as experience (see Table 1.2).

Table A6.1 *APM taxonomy range 1: technical competences*

Technical competence		Knowledge											Experience										
		0	1	2	3	4	5	6	7	8	9	10	0	1	2	3	4	5	6	7	8	9	10
TC01	Concept						D	C	B	A	A	A	D	D	D	D	D	C	B	A	A	A	A
TC02	Project success and benefits management					D	D	C	B	A	A	A	D	D	D	D	D	C	C	B	A	A	A
TC03	Stakeholder management					D	C	C	B	A	A	A	D	D	D	D	D	C	C	B	A	A	A
TC04	Requirements management						D	C	B	A	A	A	D	D	D	D	C	C	B	A	A	A	A
TC05	Project risk management						D	C	B	A	A	A	D	D	D	D	C	C	B	A	A	A	A
TC06	Estimating		D	D	D	D	C	B	A	A	A	A	D	D	D	D	D	C	B	A	A	A	A
TC07	Business case		D	D	D	D	C	B	A	A	A	A	D	D	D	D	D	C	B	A	A	A	A
TC08	Marketing and sales		D	D	D	D	C	B	B	A	A	A	D	D	D	D	C	B	B	A	A	A	A
TC09	Project reviews		D	D	D	D	C	C	B	A	A	A	D	D	D	D	C	C	B	B	A	A	A
TC10	Definition		D	D	D	D	D	C	B	A	A	A	D	D	D	D	C	B	B	A	A	A	A
TC11	Scope management						D	C	B	A	A	A	D	D	D	D	C	B	B	A	A	A	A
TC12	Modelling and testing		D	D	D	C	B	B	A	A	A	A	D	D	D	C	B	B	A	A	A	A	A
TC13	Methods and procedures		D	D	D	D	C	B	A	A	A	A	D	D	D	C	C	B	B	A	A	A	A
TC14	Project quality management						D	C	B	A	A	A	D	D	D	D	C	C	B	A	A	A	A
TC15	Scheduling						D	C	B	A	A	A	D	D	D	D	D	C	B	A	A	A	A
TC16	Resource management					D	C	B	A	A	A	A	D	D	D	D	C	C	B	A	A	A	A
TC17	Information management and reporting					D	C	B	A	A	A	A	D	D	D	D	C	C	B	A	A	A	A
TC18	Project management plan		D	D	D	D	C	C	B	A	A	A	D	D	D	D	C	C	B	B	A	A	A
TC19	Configuration management					D	C	C	B	A	A	A	D	D	D	D	C	C	B	A	A	A	A
TC20	Change control					D	C	C	B	A	A	A	D	D	D	D	C	C	B	A	A	A	A
TC21	Implementation					D	C	B	A	A	A	A	D	D	D	C	C	B	B	A	A	A	A
TC22	Technology management			D	C	B	B	A	A	A	A	A	D	D	D	C	B	B	A	A	A	A	A
TC23	Budgeting and cost management						D	C	B	A	A	A	D	D	D	D	D	C	B	A	A	A	A
TC24	Procurement					D	C	C	B	A	A	A	D	D	D	D	C	B	A	A	A	A	A
TC25	Issue management						D	C	B	A	A	A	D	D	D	D	C	C	B	A	A	A	A
TC26	Development		D	D	D	C	B	B	A	A	A	A	D	D	D	C	B	B	A	A	A	A	A
TC27	Value management		D	D	D	C	B	B	A	A	A	A	D	D	D	C	C	B	B	A	A	A	A
TC28	Earned value management		D	D	D	D	C	B	B	A	A	A	D	D	D	D	C	C	B	B	A	A	A
TC29	Value engineering		D	D	D	C	B	B	A	A	A	A	D	D	D	C	C	B	B	A	A	A	A
TC30	Handover and closeout						D	C	B	A	A	A	D	D	D	D	D	C	B	A	A	A	A

Table A6.2 *APM taxonomy range 2: behavioural competences*

Behavioural competence		Knowledge											Experience										
		0	1	2	3	4	5	6	7	8	9	10	0	1	2	3	4	5	6	7	8	9	10
BC01	Communication						D	C	B	A	A	A	D	D	D	D	D	C	B	B	A	A	A
BC02	Teamwork						D	C	B	A	A	A	D	D	D	D	D	C	B	A	A	A	A
BC03	Leadership				D	C	C	B	A	A	A	A	D	D	D	D	C	C	B	B	A	A	A
BC04	Conflict management					D	C	B	A	A	A	A	D	D	D	D	D	C	C	B	A	A	A
BC05	Negotiation					D	C	B	A	A	A	A	D	D	D	D	C	C	C	B	A	A	A
BC06	Human resource management				D	C	B	A	A	A	A	A	D	D	D	C	B	B	A	A	A	A	A
BC07	Behavioural characteristics				D	D	C	B	A	A	A	A	D	D	D	D	C	C	B	A	A	A	A
BC08	Learning and development		D	D	D	C	B	B	A	A	A	A	D	D	C	C	C	B	A	A	A	A	A
BC09	Professionalism and ethics					D	C	B	A	A	A	A	D	D	D	D	C	C	B	A	A	A	A

Table A6.3 *APM taxonomy range 3: contextual competences*

Contextual competence		Knowledge											Experience										
		0	1	2	3	4	5	6	7	8	9	10	0	1	2	3	4	5	6	7	8	9	10
CC01	Project sponsorship				D	D	C	C	B	A	A	A	D	D	D	D	C	B	B	A	A	A	A
CC02	Health, safety and environmental management				D	C	B	A	A	A	A	A	D	D	D	C	C	B	A	A	A	A	A
CC03	Project life cycles					D	C	B	A	A	A	A	D	D	D	D	C	C	B	A	A	A	A
CC04	Project finance and funding				D	C	B	A	A	A	A	A	D	D	D	C	C	B	A	A	A	A	A
CC05	Legal awareness					D	C	B	A	A	A	A	D	D	D	C	B	B	A	A	A	A	A
CC06	Organisational roles					D	C	B	A	A	A	A	D	D	D	C	B	B	A	A	A	A	A
CC07	Organisation structure						D	C	B	A	A	A	D	D	D	D	C	C	B	B	A	A	A
CC08	Governance of project management		D	D	D	D	C	B	A	A	A	A	D	D	D	D	C	C	B	B	A	A	A

Table A6.4 *Percentage weighting of competence domains at APM Levels A, B, C, D*

Competence domain	APM Level A	APM Level B	APM Level C	APM Level D
Behavioural	30	25	20	15
Contextual	30	25	20	15

Table A6.5 *Knowledge and experience average scores required at each APM Level (range 0–10)*

Components of competence	APM Level A	APM Level B	APM Level C	APM Level D
Knowledge	7	6	5	4
Experience	7	6	4	0

BIBLIOGRAPHY AND FURTHER READING

1. Caupin, G., Knoepfel, H., Koch, G., Pannenbacker, K., Perez-Polo, F., Seabury, C. (2006) *ICB-IPMA Competence Baseline*, version 3.0, International Project Management Association, Nijkerk, Netherlands, ISBN 0-9553213-0-1 *and also*: www.ipma.ch/Pages/IPMA.aspx

2. IPMA (2007) *ICRG-IPMA Certification Regulations and Guidelines*, version 3.0, International Project Management Association, Nijkerk, Netherlands

3. Association for Project Management (2006) *APM Body of Knowledge*, 5th edn, APM, High Wycombe, ISBN 978-1-903494-13-4

4. Project Management Institute (2004) *Guide to the Project Management Body of Knowledge*, Project Management Institute, USA

5. Australian Institute for Project Management (2004) *National Competency Standards for Project Management*, AIPM, Sydney, Australia, www.aipm. com.au/html/ncspm.cfm

6. Fangel, Morten (ed.) on behalf of the Association of Danish Project Management, the Norwegian Association of Project Management and the Swedish Project Management Society (2005) *Competencies in Project Management: National Competence Baseline for Scandinavia*, Association of Danish Project Management, Hilleroed, Denmark, ISBN 87-985726-8-7

7. Stevens, M. (ed.) (2002) *Project Management Pathways*, APM, High Wycombe, ISBN 978-1-903494-01-1

8. ECITB (2003) *National Occupational Standards for Project Management*, version 1.01 – www.ecitb.org.uk *and also*: www.apm.org.uk/page.asp? categoryID = 4

9. Global Alliance for Project Performance Standards – www.globalpmstandards.org (GAPPS)

10. India: National Competence Baseline, June 2005

11. USA: ASAPM National Competence Baseline, version 1.0, October 2005 – www.pmcert.org/cert_NCB.asp

12. Ireland: National Competence Baseline for Ireland, version 1.0, 2001 – www.projectmanagement.ie

13. Level D syllabus and Candidate Guidance Notes – www.apm.org.uk/APMP. asp

14. Level C Candidate Guidance Notes – www.apm.org.uk/Practitioner Qualification.asp

15. Level B guidance – www.apm.org.uk/CertificatedProjectManager.asp

16. BS 6079-1: 2002 Project Management, Guide to Project Management, ISBN 0-580 397-16-5–www.bsi-global.com

GLOSSARY OF PROJECT MANAGEMENT TERMS

This glossary contains terms used in the fifth edition of the *APM Body of Knowledge*, and many other terms used in the wider application of project management. Terms in bold within the definition are also listed.

Accept To make a response to a risk (**threat** or **opportunity**) where no course of action is taken.

Acceptance The formal process of accepting delivery of a **deliverable** or a product.

Acceptance criteria The requirements and essential conditions that have to be achieved before project deliverables are accepted.

Acceptance test* A formal, predefined test conducted to determine the compliance of the **deliverable(s)** with the **acceptance criteria**.

Accrual Work done for which payment is due but has not been made.

Accrued costs* Costs that are earmarked for the project and for which payment is due, but has not been made.

Acquisition strategy The establishment of the most appropriate means of procuring the component parts or services of a project.

Activity* A task, job, operation or process consuming time and possibly other re-sources. (The smallest self-contained unit of work used to define the logic of a project.)

Activity duration The length of time that it takes to complete an activity.

Activity ID A unique code identifying each activity in a project.

Activity network *See* **network diagram**.

Activity-on-arrow network* Arrow diagram – a **network diagram** in which the arrows symbolise the activities.

Activity-on-node network* Precedence diagram – a **network diagram** in which the nodes symbolise the activities.

Activity status The state of completion of an activity.

Actual cost* The incurred costs that are charged to the project budget and for which payment has been made or accrued.

Actual cost of work performed (ACWP)* A term used in **earned value management** for the cumulative cost of work accrued on the

---

*Asterisks indicate definitions that are also published in BS6079-2:2000. Permission to reproduce extracts of BS6079-2:2000 is granted by BSI. British Standards can be obtained from BSI customer services, 389 Chiswick High Road, London, W4 4AL, tel.: +44 (0)20 8996 9001. Email: cservices@bsi-global.com.

project in a specific period or up to a specific stage. Note: for some purposes cost may be measured in labour hours rather than money. *See* **actual cost.**

Actual dates The dates on which activities started and finished, as opposed to planned or forecast dates.

Actual expenditure The money that has already been paid.

Actual finish The date on which an activity was completed.

Actual start The date on which an activity was started.

Actual time expended The elapsed time from the beginning of an activity to date.

Adjudication The legal process by which an arbiter or other independent third party reviews evidence and argumentation, including legal reasoning, set forth by opposing parties to come to a decision or judgement which determines rights and obligations between the parties involved.

Agile development A family of methodologies where the development emphasises real time communication and software.

Alliancing An arrangement whereby two or more organisations agree to manage a contract or range of contracts between them jointly. *See* **partnering.**

Alternative dispute resolution (ADR) The collective term for settling disputes with the help of an independent third party without a court hearing. For example **arbitration, adjudication** and **mediation.**

Arbitration The process of using a third party appointed to settle a **dispute.**

Arrow diagram* *See* **activity-on-arrow network.**

Arrow diagram method (ADM) A convention used to represent an activity in a **network diagram.** Also known as activity-on-arrow method.

As late as possible (ALAP) An activity for which the early start date is set as late as possible without delaying the early dates of any successor.

As soon as possible (ASAP) An activity for which the early start date is set to be as soon as possible. This is the default activity type in most project scheduling systems.

Associated revenue* That part of a project cost that is of a revenue nature and therefore charged as incurred to the profit and loss account.

Assumptions Statements that will be taken for granted as fact and upon which the project business case will be justified.

Assurance The process of examining with the intent to verify. *See* **quality assurance.**

Audit* The systematic retrospective examination of the whole, or part, of a project or function to measure conformance with predetermined standards.

Authorisation points The points at which the business case is reviewed and approved.

Avoid To respond to a **threat** in a way that eliminates its probability or impact on the project.

Backward pass* A procedure whereby the latest event times or the latest finish and start times for the activities of a network are calculated.

Balanced matrix An organisational matrix where functions and projects have the same priority.

Bar chart* A chart on which activities and their durations are represented by lines drawn to a common timescale. *See* **Gantt chart.**

Base date A reference date used as a basis for the start of a project calendar.

Baseline* The reference levels against which the project is monitored and controlled.

Baseline cost(s) The amount of money a project or activity was intended to cost when the project plan was baselined.

Baseline date(s) The original planned start and finish dates for a project or an activity when the schedule was baselined.

Baseline plan The fixed **project plan**. It is the standard by which performance against the project plan is measured.

Baseline schedule The fixed **project schedule**. It is the standard by which project schedule performance is measured.

Behavioural characteristics The elements that separate and describe a person's preferred way of acting, interacting and reacting in a variety of situations.

Benchmarking A review of what other organisations are doing in the same area. Those organisations that appear to be particularly successful in what they do and how they do it are taken to be examples to be emulated, i.e. used as benchmarks.

Benefit The quantifiable and measurable improvement resulting from completion of project **deliverables** that is perceived as positive by a **stakeholder**. It will normally have a tangible value, expressed in monetary terms, that will justify the investment.

Benefits framework An outline of the expected benefits of the project (or **programme**), the business operations affected, and current and target performance measures. The totality of plans and arrangements to enable the organisation to realise the defined benefits from a project or programme of projects.

Benefits management The identification of the benefits (of a **project** or **programme**) at an organisational level, and the tracking and realisation of those benefits.

Benefits management plan A plan that specifies who is responsible for achieving the benefits set out in the **benefits profile** and how achievement of the benefits is to be measured, managed and monitored.

Benefits profile A representation of when the benefits are planned to be realised.

Benefits realisation The practice of ensuring that the outcome of a project produces the projected benefits.

Benefits realisation review A review undertaken after a period of operation of the project **deliverables**. It is intended to establish that project benefits have been or are being realised.

Bid A tender, quotation or any offer to enter into a contract.

Bid analysis An analysis of bids or tenders.

Bid list A list of contractors or suppliers invited to submit bids for goods or services.

Bidding The process of preparing and submitting a bid or tender.

Blueprint A document defining and describing what a **programme** is designed to achieve in terms of the business vision and the operational vision.

Body of knowledge An inclusive term that describes the sum of knowledge within the profession of **project management**. As with other professions, such as law and medicine, the body of knowledge rests with the practitioners and academics that apply and advance it.

Bond Security against a loan or investment.

Bottleneck A process constraint that determines the capacity or capability of a system and restricts the rate, volume or flow of a process.

Bottom-up estimating An estimating technique based on making estimates for every work package (or activity) in the **work breakdown structure**, and summarising them to provide a total estimate of cost or effort required.

Brainstorming The unstructured generation of ideas by a group of people in a short space of time.

Branching logic* Conditional logic. Alternative paths in a **probabilistic network**.

Breaches of contract A legal concept in which a binding agreement (contract) is not honoured by one of the parties to the contract, by non-performance or interference with the other party's performance.

Breakdown structure A hierarchical structure by which project elements are broken down, or decomposed. *See* **cost breakdown structure (CBS)**, **organisational breakdown structure (OBS)**, **product breakdown structure (PBS)**, **risk breakdown structure (RBS)** and **work breakdown structure (WBS)**.

Brief A high-level outline (strategic specification) of **stakeholder** (customer/client) needs and requirements for a project.

Budget* The agreed cost of the project or a quantification of resources needed to achieve an activity by a set time within which the activity owners are required to work.

Budget at completion (BAC) The sum total of the time-phased budgets.

Budget cost The cost anticipated at the start of a project.

Budget elements The resources, people, materials or other entities needed to do the work. They are typically assigned to a **work package**, but can also be defined at the **cost account** level.

Budget estimate An approximate estimate prepared in the early stages of a project to establish financial viability or to secure resources.

Budgeted cost of work performed (BCWP) A term used in **earned value management**. The planned cost of work completed to date. BCWP is also the 'earned value' of work completed to date. *See* **earned value**.

Budgeted cost of work scheduled (BCWS) A term used in **earned value management**. The planned cost of work that should have been achieved according to the project **baseline** dates. *See* **planned cost**.

Budgeting Time-phased financial requirements.

Budgeting and cost management The estimating of costs and the setting of an agreed budget, and the management of actual and forecast costs against that budget.

Buffer A term used in **critical chain** for the centralised management of **contingencies**.

Build, own, operate, transfer (BOOT) A situation whereby a private operator builds, owns, operates and then transfers a facility to another party after a specific period.

Build (stage) A stage within the **implementation** phase where the project **deliverables** are built or constructed.

Business-as-usual An organisation's normal day-to-day operations.

Business case The documented justification for undertaking a project, in terms of evaluating the benefit, cost and risk of alternative options and the rationale for the preferred solution. Its purpose is to obtain management commitment and approval for investment in the project. The business case is owned by the **sponsor**.

Business change manager(s) The role responsible for **benefits management** from identification through to realisation, and ensuring the implementation and embedding of the new capabilities delivered by projects. May be more than one individual.

Business objectives The overall objectives of the business, as opposed to the project.

Business risk assessment The assessment of risk to business objectives rather than risk to achieving project objectives.

Business to business (B2B) The exchange of services, information and products from a business to another business – generally undertaken electronically using the World Wide Web.

Business to consumer (B2C) The exchange of services, information and products from a business to a consumer – generally undertaken electronically using the World Wide Web.

Calendar A list of time intervals for the project in which activities or resources can or cannot be scheduled. A project usually has one default calendar for the normal workweek (Monday to Friday, for example), but may have other calendars as well. Each calendar can be customised with its own holidays and extra work days. Resources and activities can be attached to any of the calendars that are defined.

Capability A project capability (or outcome) that enables a benefit to be achieved. Alternatively, the necessary attributes to perform or accomplish.

Capability maturity models An organisational model that describes a number of evolutionary levels in which an organisation manages its processes, from ad hoc use of processes to continual improvement of its processes.

Capital Monetary investment in the project. Alternatively, wealth used or available for use in the production of more wealth.

Capital cost* The carrying cost in a balance sheet of acquiring an asset and bringing it to the point where it is capable of performing its intended function over a future series of periods. *See* **revenue cost**.

Capital employed* The amount of investment in an organisation or project, normally the sum of fixed and current assets, less current liabilities at a particular date.

Capital expenditure (CapEX) The long-term expenditure for property, plant and equipment.

Cash flow* Cash receipts and payments in a specified period.

Cash flow forecast A prediction of the difference between cash received and payments to be made during a specific period or for the duration of the project.

Central repository A central location where data and information are stored. This can be a physical location, such as a filing cabinet, or a virtual location, such as a dedicated drive on a computer system.

Champion An end-user representative often seconded into a **project team**. Someone who acts as an advocate for a proposal or project. Someone who spearheads an idea or action and 'sells it' throughout the organisation. A person within the parent organisation who promotes and defends a project.

Change A change to a project's baseline **scope**, cost, time or quality objectives.

Change authority An organisation or individual with power to authorise changes to a project.

Change control A process that ensures that all changes made to a project's baseline **scope**, cost, time or quality objectives are identified, evaluated, approved, rejected or deferred.

Change control board A formally constituted group of **stakeholders** responsible for approving or rejecting changes to the project **baselines**.

Change freeze A point on a project after which no further changes will be considered.

Change log A record of all project changes proposed, authorised, rejected or deferred.

Change management The formal process through which changes to the project plan are approved and introduced. Also the process by which organisational change is introduced.

Change register *See* **change log**.

Change request A request to obtain formal approval for changes to the **scope**, design, methods, costs or planned aspects of a project.

Charter A document that sets out the working relationships and agreed behaviours within a **project team**.

Claim A written demand or assertion by a contracting party seeking as a matter of right financial adjustment or interpretation of an existing contract subject to the terms of the contract's dispute clause.

Client The party to a contract who commissions work and pays for it on completion.

Client brief *See* **brief**.

Closeout The process of finalising all project matters, carrying out final project reviews, archiving project information and redeploying the remaining project team. *See* **handover** and **closeout**.

Closure The formal end point of a project, either because it has been completed or because it has been terminated early.

Code of accounts Any numbering system, usually based on corporate code of accounts of the primary performing organ-

isation, used to monitor project costs by category.

Commissioning* The advancement of an installation from the stage of static completion to full working order and achievement of the specified operational requirements. *See* **mechanical completion** and **pre-commissioning**.

Commitment A binding financial obligation, typically in the form of a purchase order or contract. The amount of money removed from the budget by this obligation.

Committed costs* Costs that are legally committed even if delivery has not taken place with invoices neither raised nor paid.

Common law The tradition, custom and especially precedent of previous judgements.

Communication The giving, receiving, processing and interpretation of information. Information can be conveyed verbally, non-verbally, actively, passively, formally, informally, consciously or unconsciously.

Communication plan A document that identifies what information is to be communicated to whom, why, when, where, how and through which medium, and the desired impact.

Communication planning The establishment of project **stakeholders'** communication and information needs.

Community of practice A special type of informal network that emerges from a desire to work more effectively or to understand work more deeply among members of a particular speciality or work group.

Comparative estimating An estimating technique based on the comparison with, and factoring from, the cost of a previous similar project or operation.

Competitive tendering A formal **procurement** process whereby vendors or contractors are given an equal chance to tender for the supply of goods or services against a fixed set of rules.

Completion A project or part of a project agreed to have been completed in accordance with all requirements.

Completion date The calculated date by which the project could finish, following careful estimating and scheduling.

Concept (phase) The first phase in the **project life cycle**. During this phase the need, opportunity or problem is confirmed, the overall feasibility of the project is considered and a preferred solution identified.

Concession The acceptance of something that is not within specified requirements.

Concurrent engineering The systematic approach to the simultaneous, integrated design of products and their related processes, such as manufacturing, testing and supporting.

Configuration* Functional and physical characteristics of a **deliverable** (product) as defined in technical documents and achieved in the product.

Configuration audit A check to ensure that all **deliverables** (products) in a project conform with one another and to the current specification. It ensures that relevant **quality assurance** procedures have been implemented and that there is consistency throughout project documentation.

Configuration control A system to ensure that all changes to **configuration** items are controlled. An important aspect is being able to identify the interrelationships between configuration items.

Configuration identification The unique identification of all items within the **configuration**. It involves breaking down the proj-

ect into component parts or configuration items, creating a unique numbering or referencing system for each item and establishing configuration **baselines**.

Configuration item A part of a **configuration** that has a set function and is designated for **configuration management**. It identifies uniquely all items within the configuration.

Configuration management* Technical and administrative activities concerned with the creation, maintenance and controlled change of configuration throughout the project or product life cycle. See BS EN ISO 10007 for guidance on configuration management, including specialist terminology.

Configuration status accounting A record and report of the current status and history of all changes to the **configuration**. It provides a complete record of what has happened to the configuration to date.

Conflict management The process of identifying and addressing differences that if unmanaged would affect **project objectives**. Effective conflict management prevents differences becoming destructive elements in a project.

Conformance audit An audit of the operation of the **programme** or project management or other process to identify whether the defined processes are being adhered to.

Consideration In contract law – something of value. It may be money, an act or a promise. It is one of the key elements required to have a binding contract.

Constraints Things that should be considered as fixed or must happen. Restrictions that will affect the project.

Consumable resource A type of resource that only remains available until consumed (for example, a material). *See* **replenishable resource**.

Context *See* **project context.**

Contingency The planned allotment of time and cost or other resources for unforeseeable risks within a project. Something held in reserve for the unknown.

Contingency budget The amount of money required to implement a **contingency plan.**

Contingency plan* Alternative course(s) of action to cope with project risks or if expected results fail to materialise.

Continuing professional development (CPD) A personal commitment made by an individual to keep their professional knowledge up to date and improve their capability, with a focus on what the person learns and how they develop throughout their career.

Continuous improvement A business philosophy popularised in Japan where it is known as *kaizen*. It creates steady growth and improvement by keeping a business focused on its goals and priorities. It is a planned systematic approach to improvement on a continual basis.

Contract A mutually binding agreement in which the contractor is obligated to provide services or products and the buyer is obligated to provide payment for them.

Contract price The price payable by the customer under the contract for the proper delivery of supplies and services specified in the **scope of work** of the contract.

Contract target cost The negotiated costs for the original defined contract and all contractual changes that have been agreed and approved, but excluding the estimated cost of any authorised, unpriced changes.

Contract target price The negotiated estimated costs plus profit or fee.

Contractor A person, company or firm that holds a contract for carrying out the works and/or the supply of goods or services in connection with the project.

Control charts Charts that display the results, over time, of a process. They are used in quality management to determine if the process is in need of adjustment.

Coordination The act of ensuring that work carried out by different organisations and in different places fits together effectively.

Corrective action Changes made to bring future project performance back into line with the plan.

Cost account A means of defining what work is to be performed, who will perform it and who is to pay for it. Another term for cost account is control account.

Cost account manager (CAM) A member of a functional organisation responsible for cost account performance, and for the management of resources to accomplish such activities.

Cost–benefit analysis* An analysis of the relationship between the costs of undertaking an activity or project, initial and recurrent, and the benefits likely to arise from the changed situation, initially and recurrently.

Cost breakdown structure* (CBS) The hierarchical breakdown of a project into cost elements.

Cost budgeting The allocation of cost estimates to individual project activities or **deliverables.**

Cost centre* A location, person, activity or project in respect of which costs may be ascertained and related to cost units.

Cost code* A unique identity for a specified element of work. A code assigned to activities that allows costs to be consolidated according to the elements of a code structure.

Cost control system Any system of keeping costs within the bounds of budgets or standards based upon work actually performed.

Cost curve A graph plotted against a horizontal timescale and cumulative cost vertical scale.

Cost estimating The process of predicting the costs of a project.

Cost incurred A cost identified through the use of the accrued method of accounting or a cost actually paid. Costs include direct labour, direct materials and all allowable indirect costs.

Cost management *See* **budgeting and cost management**.

Cost performance index (CPI)* A term used in **earned value management**. A measure expressed as a percentage or other ratio of actual cost to budget plan. The ratio of work accomplished versus work cost incurred for a specified time period. The CPI is an efficiency rating for work accomplished for resources expended.

Cost performance report A regular cost report to reflect cost and schedule status information for management.

Cost plan A budget that shows the amounts and expected dates of costs being incurred by the project or contract.

Cost plus fixed fee contract A type of contract where the buyer reimburses the seller for the seller's allowable costs plus a fixed fee.

Cost plus incentive fee contract A type of contract where the buyer reimburses the seller for the seller's allowable costs and the seller earns a profit if defined criteria are met.

Cost-reimbursement type contracts A category of contracts based on payments to a contractor for allowable estimated costs, usually requiring only a 'best efforts' performance standard from the contractor.

Cost/schedule planning and control specification (C/SPCS) The US Air Force initiative in the mid-1960s which later resulted in their cost/schedule control systems criteria, C/SCSC.

Cost–time resource sheet (CTR) A document that describes each major element in the **work breakdown structure** (WBS), including a **statement of work** (SOW) describing the work content, resources required, the time frame of the work element and a cost estimate.

Cost variance* A term used in **earned value management**. The difference (positive or negative) between the actual expenditure and the planned/budgeted expenditure.

Critical activity An activity that has **zero float** or **negative float**. Alternatively an activity that has the lowest float on the project.

Critical chain A networking technique based on Goldratt's **theory of constraints** that identifies paths through a project based on resource dependencies as well as technological precedence requirements.

Critical path* A sequence of activities through a project network from start to finish, the sum of whose durations determines the overall project duration. There may be more than one such path. The path through a series of activities, taking into account interdependencies, in which the late completion of activities will have an impact on the project end date or delay a **key milestone**.

Critical path analysis* (CPA) The procedure for calculating the **critical path** and **floats** in a network.

Critical path method (CPM) A technique used to predict project duration by analysing which sequence of activities has the least amount of scheduling flexibility.

Critical success factor *See* **success factors.**

Criticality index Used in **risk analysis**, a representation of the percentage of **simulation** trials that resulted in the activity being placed on the critical path.

Culture The attitudes and values that inform those involved in a project.

Current dates The planned start and finish dates for an activity according to the current schedule.

Cut-off date The end date of a reporting period.

Dangle An activity in a **network diagram** that has either no predecessors or no successors. If neither, it is referred to as an isolated activity.

Decision tree A pictorial (tree-like) representation of the alternatives and outcomes in a decision situation.

Definition (phase) The second phase of the **project life cycle.** During this phase the preferred solution is further evaluated and optimised. Often an iterative process, definition can affect requirements and the project's scope, time, cost and quality objectives.

Delegation The practice of getting others to perform work effectively that one chooses not to do oneself. The process by which authority and responsibility is distributed from **project manager** to subordinates.

Deliverables* The end products of a project or the measurable results of intermediate activities within the project organisation. *See* **product.**

Delphi technique A process where a consensus view is reached by consultation with experts, often used as an estimating technique.

Demobilisation The controlled dispersal of personnel when they are no longer needed on a project.

Dependencies* Something on which successful delivery of the project critically depends, which may often be outside the sphere of influence of the **project manager** – for example, another project. Alternatively, dependency, a precedence relationship: a restriction that means that one activity has to precede, either in part or in total, another activity.

Dependency arrow* A link arrow used in an **activity-on-node network** to represent the interrelationships of activities in a project.

Design authority The person or organisation with overall design responsibility for the products of the project.

Design (stage) A stage within the **implementation** phase where the design of project **deliverables** is finalised.

Detailed design The in-depth design of the chosen solution, ready for full implementation.

Deterministic Something that is predetermined, with no possibility of an alternative outcome.

Deterministic estimate A predetermined estimate with no possibility of an alternative outcome.

Development The working up of a preferred solution to an optimised solution during the **definition** and **implementation** phases of a project.

Deviations Departure from the established plan or requirements.

Direct costs* Costs that are specifically attributable to an activity or group of activities without apportionment. The cost of resources expended in the achievement of work that are directly charged to a project, without the inclusion of **indirect costs**.

Direct labour Labour that is specifically identified with a particular activity. It is incurred for the exclusive benefit of the project.

Discipline An area of expertise. *See* **function.**

Discounted cash flow (DCF)* The concept of relating future cash inflows and outflows over the life of a project or operation to a common base value, thereby allowing more validity to comparison of projects with different durations and rates of cash flow.

Dispute A disagreement between parties concerning a particular event.

Dispute resolution The process of resolving disputes between parties.

'Do nothing' option The result or consequence of taking no action, i.e., doing nothing to correct a problem, satisfy a need or seize an opportunity.

Drawdown The removal of funds from an agreed source resulting in a reduction of available funds.

Dummy activity (in activity-on-arrow network) A logical link that may require time but no other resource. An activity representing no actual work to be done but required for reasons of logic or nomenclature.

Duration The length of time needed to complete the project or an activity.

Duration compression Often resulting in an increase in cost, the shortening of a project schedule without reducing the project **scope.**

Duty of care The obligation to persons who are so closely and directly affected by an individual's acts that the individual ought

reasonably to have had them in contemplation as being affected when considering acts or omissions that are subsequently called into question.

Dynamic systems development method (DSDM) A non-proprietary, **agile development** method for developing business solutions within tight timeframes, commonly used in IT projects.

Earliest finish date The earliest possible date by which an activity can finish within the logical and imposed constraints of the network.

Earliest start date The earliest possible date when an activity can start within the logical and imposed constraints of the network.

Earned hours The time in standard hours credited as a result of the completion of a given activity or a group of activities.

Earned value* The value of the useful work done at any given point in a project. The value of completed work expressed in terms of the budget assigned to that work. A measure of project progress. Note: the budget may be expressed in cost or labour hours.

Earned value analysis An analysis of project progress where the actual money and hours (or other measure) budgeted and spent are compared to the value of the work achieved.

Earned value management A project control process based on a structured approach to planning, cost collection and performance measurement. It facilitates the integration of project **scope**, time and cost objectives, and the establishment of a **baseline plan** for performance measurement.

E-commerce Business that is conducted over the Internet using any of the applications that rely on the Web, such as e-mail, instant messaging, shopping carts and Web services.

Effectiveness A measure of how well an action meets its intended requirements.

Effort The number of labour units necessary to complete the work. Effort is usually expressed in labour hours, labour days or labour weeks and should not be confused with **duration**.

Effort-driven activity An activity whose duration is governed by resource usage and availability.

Effort remaining The estimate of **effort** remaining to complete an activity.

EFQM Excellence Model The European Foundation for Quality Management model for assessing organisational excellence.

Elapsed time The total number of calendar days (excluding non-work days such as weekends or holidays) that is needed to complete an activity.

End activity An activity with no logical successors.

End user The person or organisation that will use the facility produced by the project or the products produced by such a facility.

Enhance To respond to an **opportunity** in a way that increases its probability or impact on the project, or both.

Environment The project environment is the context within which the project is formulated, assessed and realised. This includes all external factors that have an impact on the project.

Escalation The process by which aspects of the project such as issues are drawn to the attention of those senior to the project manager, such as the sponsor, steering group or project board.

Estimate An approximation of project time and cost targets, refined throughout the **project life cycle**.

Estimate at completion (EAC) A value expressed in money and/or hours to represent the projected final costs of work when completed, also referred to as projected **out-turn cost**.

Estimated cost to complete (ECC) The value expressed in either money or hours developed to represent the cost of the work required to complete an activity.

Estimating The use of a range of tools and techniques to produce estimates.

Ethical procurement Procurement that is in accordance with established ethics or moral values.

Event* The state in the progress of a project after the completion of all preceding activities, but before the start of any succeeding activity. A defined point that is the beginning or end of an activity.

Exception management An approach to management that focuses on drawing attention to instances where planned and actual results are expected to be, or are already, significantly different. Exceptions can be better than planned or worse than planned.

Exception report* A focused report drawing attention to instances where planned and actual results are expected to be, or are already, significantly different.

Exceptions Occurrences that cause deviation from a plan, such as **issues, change requests** and **risks**. Exceptions can also refer to items where the **cost variance** and **schedule variance** exceed predefined thresholds.

Expected monetary value The product of an event's probability of occurrence and the (financial) gain or loss that will result. Hence if there is a 50% probability of rain and the rain will result in a £1000 increase in cost, the EMV will be $0.5 \times £1000$, i.e. £500.

Expediting The facilitation and acceleration of progress by the removal of obstacles (particularly used in **procurement management**).

Expended hours The hours spent to achieve an activity or group of activities.

Expenditure A charge against available funds, evidenced by a voucher, claim or other document. Expenditures represent the actual payment of funds.

Exploit To respond to an **opportunity** in a way that maximises both its probability and impact on the project.

Extended life cycle A **project life cycle** model that includes the operational life and termination, including disposal of the project **deliverables**.

External constraint A **constraint** from outside the project.

External environment The environment in which the project must be undertaken that is external to the organisation carrying out the project.

External suppliers Suppliers external to the organisation carrying out the project.

Facility The final result, outcome or **deliverable** of the project.

Factors Situations that affect or influence outcomes.

Fast-tracking* The process of reducing the duration of a project usually by overlapping phases or activities that were originally planned to be done sequentially. The process of reducing the number of sequential relationships and replacing them typically with parallel relationships, usually to achieve shorter overall durations but often with increased risk.

Feasibility study* An analysis to determine if a course of action is possible within the terms of reference of the project. Work carried out on a proposed project or alterna-

tives to provide a basis for deciding whether or not to proceed.

Final account The account that finally closes a purchase order or contract.

Financial appraisal An assessment of the financial aspects of a project or programme.

Finance and funding *See* **project financing and funding**.

Finish-to-finish lag The minimum amount of time that must pass between the finish of one activity and the finish of its successor(s).

Finish-to-start lag The minimum amount of time that must pass between the finish of one activity and the start of its successor(s).

Firm fixed-price contract A contract where the buyer pays a set amount to the seller regardless of that seller's cost to complete the contract.

Fitness for purpose The degree to which the project management process and project deliverables satisfy stakeholder needs. *See* **quality**.

Fixed date A calendar date (associated with a schedule) that cannot be moved or changed during the project.

Fixed-price contracts A generic category of contracts based on the establishment of firm legal commitments to complete the required work. A performing contractor is legally obligated to finish the job, no matter how much it costs to complete.

Float *See* **free float** and **total float**.

Flow diagram A graphic representation of workflow and the logical sequence of the work elements without regard to a timescale. It is used to show the logic associated with a process rather than duration for completion of work.

Force-field analysis A technique used to identify the various pressures promoting or resisting change.

Forecast Estimates or prediction of future conditions and events based on information and knowledge available when the estimate was prepared.

Forecast costs A projection of future costs that the project will incur.

Forecast final cost *See* **estimate at completion**.

Forecast out-turn cost The cost of actual expenditure, accruals and the estimate of the costs to complete the work to the end of the project.

Form of contract The type of contract to be used. This could be a standard form of contract relevant to the business or industry sector.

Forward pass* A procedure whereby the earliest event times or the earliest start and finish times for the activities of a network are calculated.

Free float* Time by which an activity may be delayed or extended without affecting the start of any succeeding activity.

Function A specialist department that provides dedicated services, for example, accounts department, production department, marketing department or IT.

Functional analysis The identification and analysis of the functional attributes of different solutions.

Functional analysis and system technique (FAST) An evolution of the value analysis process. FAST permits people with different technical backgrounds to effectively communicate and resolve issues that require multidisciplined considerations. It builds on value analysis by linking the simply expressed, verb–noun functions to describe complex systems.

Functional departments *See* **function**.

Functional manager The person responsible for the business and technical management of a functional group.

Functional organisation (structure) A functional management structure where specific functions of a business are grouped into specialist departments that provide a dedicated service to the whole of the organisation, for example, accounts department, production department, marketing department or IT.

Functional specification A document specifying in some detail the functions that are required of a system and the constraints that will apply.

Funding The actual money available for expenditure on the project.

Funding profile An estimate of funding requirements over time.

Gantt chart* A particular type of **bar chart** used in project management showing planned activity against time. A Gantt chart is a time-phased graphic display of activity durations. Activities are listed with other tabular information on the left side with time intervals over the bars. Activity durations are shown in the form of horizontal bars.

Gate review A formal point in a project where its expected worth, progress, cost and execution plan are reviewed and a decision is made whether to continue with the next phase or stage of the project.

Goal A one-sentence definition of specifically what will be accomplished, incorporating an event signifying completion.

Gold plating Completing deliverables to a higher specification than required to achieve acceptance criteria. Exceeding specification or grade and therefore adding cost that does not contribute to value.

Governance of project management (GoPM) Corporate governance that is specifically related to project activities. Effective governance of project management ensures that an organisation's project portfolio is aligned to the organisation's objectives, is delivered efficiently and is sustainable.

Guarantees Legally enforceable assurance of performance of a contract by a supplier or contractor.

Hammock* An activity joining two specified points that span two or more activities. Its duration is initially unspecified and is determined only by the durations of the specified activities. A group of activities, **milestones** or other hammocks aggregated together for analysis or reporting purposes. This term is sometimes used to describe an activity such as management support that has no duration of its own but derives one from the time difference between the two points to which it is connected.

Handover The point in the **project life cycle** where **deliverables** are handed over to the **sponsor** and **users**. *See* **handover and closeout**.

Handover and closeout (phase) The fourth and final phase in the **project life cycle**, during which final project **deliverables** are handed over to the **sponsor** and **users**. Closeout is the process of finalising all project matters, carrying out final project reviews, archiving project information and redeploying the project team.

Hazards Potential sources of harm.

Health and safety plan The plan that identifies the health and safety strategies and procedures to be used on the project.

Health and safety risk assessment A legislative requirement placed on all employers and the self-employed.

Health, safety and environmental management The process of determining and applying appropriate standards and methods to minimise the likelihood of accidents, injuries or environmental damage both during the project and during the operation of its **deliverables**.

Hierarchical coding structure A coding system that can be represented as a multi-level tree structure in which every code except those at the top of the tree has a parent code.

Hierarchy of networks* Range of networks (**network diagrams**) at different levels of detail, from summary down to working levels, showing the relationships between those networks.

High-level requirements A high-level statement of the need that a project has to satisfy.

Histogram A graphic display of planned and/or actual resource usage over a period of time. It is in the form of a vertical **bar chart**, the height of each bar representing the quantity of resource usage in a given time unit. Bars may be single or multiple, or show stacked resources.

Holiday An otherwise valid working day that has been designated as exempt from work.

Human resource management (HRM) The understanding and application of the policy and procedures that directly affect the people working in the **project team** and **working group**.

Hypercritical activities Activities on the **critical path** with **negative float**.

Idea development The development of evaluated opportunities to understand their benefits and costs.

Idea evaluation The ranking of identified opportunities according to their appropriateness.

Impact The assessment of the effect on an objective of a risk occurring.

Impact analysis An assessment of the merits of pursuing a particular course of action or of the potential impact of a requested change.

Implementation (phase) The third phase of the **project life cycle** where the **project management plan** (PMP) is executed, monitored and controlled. During this phase the design is finalised and used to build the **deliverables**.

Imposed date* A point in time determined by external circumstances.

Imposed finish A finish date imposed on an activity by external circumstances or constraints.

Imposed start A start date imposed on an activity by external circumstances or constraints.

In-progress activity An activity that has been started, but not yet completed.

Incentive A contribution to motivation (usually in the form of financial or other reward).

Incurred costs* The sum of actual and committed costs, whether invoiced/paid or not, at a specified time.

Indirect cost* Costs associated with a project that cannot be directly attributed to an activity or group of activities. Resources expended that are not directly identified to any specific contract, project, product or service, such as overheads and general administration.

Influence diagram A pictorial representation of the logic and sequence with which a set of variables have an effect on one another.

Information management The collection, storage, dissemination, archiving and appropriate destruction of project information.

Initiation The process of committing the organisation to begin a project. The beginning of a project at which point certain management activities are required to ensure that the project is established with clear reference terms and adequate management structure.

Integrated baseline review (IBR) A review held following the establishment of the initial **baseline**.

Integration The process of bringing people, activities and other things together to perform effectively.

Intellectual property rights (IPR) The rights associated with intangible property that is the result of creativity.

Interdependencies An aspect of programme and portfolio management. The management of dependencies between projects, and projects and business-as-usual activities.

Interface management The management of the relationships between the work of different departments or organisations on a project or between the project and external organisations.

Interface management plan A plan identifying the interfaces internal and external to the projects and showing how they are to be managed.

Internal environment The environment in which the project must be undertaken that is internal to the organisation carrying out the project.

Internal rate of return (IRR)* A discount rate at which the **net present value** of a future cash flow is zero. Note: IRR is a special case of the **discounted cash flow** procedures.

Interrelationship The relationship between activities that need to be managed by a team or by a single person.

Investment The outlay of money or time usually for income, profit or other benefit, such as the capital outlay for a project.

Investment appraisal The appraisal of the value of a project.

Invitation to tender (ITT) An invitation to a supplier to tender or bid for the supply of goods or services.

Island of stability A review point at the end of a programme **tranche** when progress is reviewed and the next tranche is planned.

Issue A threat to the **project objectives** that cannot be resolved by the **project manager**.

Issue log A log of all **issues** raised during a project or programme, showing details of each issue, its evaluation, what decisions were made and its current status.

Issue management The process by which concerns that threaten the **project objectives** and cannot be resolved by the **project manager** can be identified and addressed to remove the threats that they pose.

Issue register *See* **issue log.**

Joint venture (JV) A joint ownership of a firm by two or more persons or other firms, or a partnership between two or more companies mutually engaged in a particular venture such as a major project.

Just in time (JIT) A philosophy in which goods, services or actions are provided on demand as needed and without waiting, queuing or storage.

Key events Major events, the achievement of which is deemed to be critical to the execution of the project.

Key events schedule *See* **master schedule.**

Key milestone A **milestone**, the achievement of which is considered to be critical to the success of the project.

Key performance indicators (KPIs) Measures of success that can be used throughout the project to ensure that it is progressing towards a successful conclusion.

Ladder* A device for representing a set of overlapping activities in a **network diagram**. The start and finish of each succeeding activity are linked to the start and finish of the preceding activity only by lead and lag activities, which consume only time.

Lag* In a **network diagram**, the minimum necessary lapse of time between the finish of one activity and the finish of an overlapping activity. The delay incurred between two specified activities.

Latest finish date The latest possible date by which an activity has to finish within the logical activity and imposed constraints of the network, without affecting the total project duration.

Latest start date The latest possible date by which an activity has to start within the logical and imposed constraints of the network, without affecting the total project duration.

Law of the land A slang term for existing laws.

Lead* In a **network diagram**, the minimum necessary lapse of time between the start of one activity and the start of an overlapping activity.

Leadership The ability to establish vision and direction, to influence and align others towards a common purpose, and to empower and inspire people to achieve project success. It enables the project to proceed in an environment of change and uncertainty.

Lean A term (applied to construction, engineering or manufacturing, for example) referring to the means by which environments can become more responsive, flexible, productive, reliable and cost-effective.

Learning and development The continual improvement of competences in the organisation. The identification and application of learning within projects develops the organisation's capability to undertake current and future projects.

Legal awareness An understanding of the relevant legal duties, rights and processes that should be applied to projects.

Legal duties The statutory laws that need to be followed and adhered to by all those involved in the project.

Lessons learned The identification of activities associated with the project that went well and those that could have been better, to recommend improvements applied in the future and to future projects.

Letter of intent A letter indicating an intent to sign a contract, usually so that work can commence prior to signing that contract.

Level one plan The master plan for the project. Level two and level three plans are given in successively more detail.

Levelling *See* **resource levelling.**

Liabilities Amounts owed under obligations for goods and services received and other assets acquired; includes accruals of amounts earned but not yet due and progress payments due on contract.

Life cycle *See* **project life cycle.**

Life cycle cost The cumulative cost of a project over its whole **life cycle.**

Linked bar chart A **bar chart** that explicitly shows the dependency links between activities.

Liquidated damages The liability in a contract to pay a specified sum for a breach of contract such as late delivery of goods or services.

Litigation Any lawsuit or other reason to resort to court to determine a legal question or matter.

Logic *See* **network logic.**

Logic diagram *See* **network diagram.**

Logical dependency A dependency between two project activities or between a project activity and a **milestone.**

Make or buy decision The decision to make a deliverable internally or to buy a finished deliverable from a supplier – for example, develop a software application in-house or purchase an existing application.

Management by exception A term used to describe management of problem or critical areas only.

Management development All aspects of staff planning, recruitment, development, training and assessment.

Management reserve* A central contingency pool. The sum of money held as an overall contingency to cover the cost impact of some unexpected event occurring.

Marketing Anticipating the demands of users, and identifying and satisfying their needs by providing the right project at the right time, cost and quality.

Master network* A network showing the complete project, from which more detailed networks are derived.

Master schedule A high-level summary **project schedule** that identifies major activities and **milestones.**

Material Property that may be incorporated into or attached to an end item to be delivered under a contract, or that may be consumed or expended in the performance of a contract.

Material take-off A list of materials required to build an item that is derived from a drawing.

Matrix organisation (structure) An organisational structure where the **project manager** and the **functional managers** share responsibility for assigning priorities and for directing the work. Individuals stay in their functional departments while performing work on one or more projects.

Maturity The sophistication and experience of an organisation in managing projects.

Mechanical completion The point at which a facility has been fully installed and individual components have been inspected and tested using safe techniques and inert materials. Ready to start **pre-commissioning** or **commissioning**.

Mediation An attempt to settle a legal dispute through active participation of a third party (mediator) who works to find points of agreement and make those in conflict agree on a fair result.

Method A consistent framework within which project management is performed.

Method statement A plan detailing how a piece of work is to be carried out.

Methods and procedures The standard practices to be used for managing projects throughout a **life cycle**.

Milestone* A key event. An event selected for its importance in the project.

Milestone plan A plan containing milestones that highlight key points of the project.

Milestone schedule A schedule that identifies the major **milestones**. *See* **master schedule**.

Mission statement A brief summary, of approximately one or two sentences, that sums up the background, purpose and benefits of the project.

Mobilisation The bringing together of project personnel and securing of equipment and facilities.

Model A way of looking at reality, usually for the purpose of abstracting and simplifying it, to make it understandable in a particular context. See **physical models**, **virtual models**.

Modelling The process of creating and using a device that duplicates the physical or operational aspects of a deliverable.

Monitoring The recording, analysing and reporting of project **performance** as compared to the plan in order to identify and report deviations.

Monte Carlo simulation A technique used to estimate the likely range of outcomes from a complex process by simulating the process under randomly selected conditions a large number of times.

Near-critical activity An activity with low **total float** that may become critical under adverse conditions.

Need, problem or opportunity The underlying reason for undertaking a project. Without a definable need, problem or opportunity, a project should not go ahead.

Negative (total) float* The time by which the duration of an activity or path has to be reduced in order to permit a limiting imposed date to be achieved.

Negotiated contract cost The estimated cost negotiated in a **cost plus fixed fee con-**

tract or the negotiated contract target cost in either a fixed-price incentive contract or a **cost plus incentive fee** contract. *See* **contract target cost.**

Negotiation A search for agreement, seeking acceptance, consensus and alignment of views. Negotiation in a project can take place on an informal basis throughout the **project life cycle**, or on a formal basis such as during **procurement**, and between signatories to a contract.

Net present value* (NPV) The aggregate of future net cash flows discounted back to a common base date, usually the present.

Network analysis* A method used for calculating a project's critical path and activity times and **floats**. *See* **critical path analysis, project network techniques.**

Network diagram A pictorial presentation of project data in which the project logic is the main determinant of the placements of the activities in the drawing. Frequently called a flowchart, PERT chart, logic drawing, activity network or logic diagram.

Network logic The collection of activity dependencies that show logical relationships between the various activities and make up a project network.

Network path *See* **path.**

Nodes* The points in a network at which arrows start and finish.

Non-recurring costs Expenditures against specific activities that are expected to occur only once on a given project.

Non-splittable activity* An activity that, once started, has to be completed to plan without interruption.

Not earlier than A restriction on an activity that indicates that it may not start or end earlier than a specified date.

Not later than A restriction on an activity that indicates that it may not start or end later than a specified date.

Objectives Predetermined results towards which effort is directed.

Operational life In an extended life cycle, part of the **operations phase**, when the deliverables are operated and maintained.

Operations phase The period during which the completed **deliverable** is used and maintained in service for its intended purpose.

Opportunity A positive risk; a risk that if it occurs will have a beneficial effect on the project. A positive aspect of project uncertainty, it may also help to negate threats.

Order of magnitude estimate An estimate carried out to give a very approximate indication of likely **out-turn costs.**

Organisation A single corporate entity that is undertaking a project or providing services to a project.

Organisation chart A graphic display of reporting relationships that provides a general framework of the organisation.

Organisation design The design of the most appropriate organisation for a project.

Organisation structure The organisational environment within which the project takes place. It defines the reporting and decision-making hierarchy of an organisation and how project management operates within it.

Organisational breakdown structure (OBS)* A hierarchical way in which the organisation may be divided into management levels and groups, for planning and control purposes.

Organisational roles The roles performed by individuals or groups in a project. Both roles and responsibilities within projects must be defined to address the transient and unique nature of projects, and to ensure that clear accountabilities can be assigned.

Original budget The initial budget established at or near the time a contract was signed or a project authorised, based on the negotiated contract cost or management's authorisation.

Original duration The duration of activities or groups of activities as recorded in the **baseline schedule**.

Other direct costs (ODC) A group of accounting elements that can be isolated to specific activities, other than labour and material. Included in ODC are such items as travel, computer time and services.

Out-of-sequence progress Progress that has been reported even though activities that have been deemed predecessors in project logic have not been completed.

Outcome The result of a project, the result of a deliberation concerning part of a project or an individual issue.

Outputs Deliverables that are the result of a process. *See* **deliverables**.

Outsourcing* The contracting-out or buying-in of facilities or work (as opposed to using in-house resources).

Out-turn cost The expected final cost of a project.

Overhead Costs incurred in the operation of a business that cannot be directly related to the individual products or services being produced. *See* **indirect cost**.

Overrun Costs incurred in excess of the contract target costs on an incentive type contract or of the estimated costs on a fixed fee contract. An overrun is that value of costs needed to complete a project, over

that value originally authorised by management.

Owner The person or organisation for which the project is ultimately undertaken and who will own, operate and benefit from the facility in the long term.

Parallel activities Two or more activities than can be done at the same time.

Parametric estimating An estimating technique that uses a statistical relationship between historic data and other variables (for example, square metreage in construction, lines of code in software development) to calculate an estimate.

Pareto diagram A **histogram** ordered by frequency of occurrence that shows how many results were generated by each identified cause.

Partnering An arrangement between two or more organisations to manage a contract between them co-operatively, as distinct from a legally established partnership. *See* **alliancing**.

Path* An activity or unbroken sequence of activities in a **network diagram**.

Payback An investment appraisal technique.

Percent complete A measure of the completion status of a partially completed activity. It may be aggregated to sections of a project or the whole project.

Performance The term used to describe the quality of the delivery and the deliverables (outputs) of the project.

Performance appraisal A review of the performance of individual people and teams on the project.

Performance management Techniques used in the management of individual and team performance. Performance management is also a term used in **earned value management** which is itself a performance management technique when applied to project performance.

Performance measurement techniques Methods used to estimate **earned value**. Different methods are appropriate to different **work packages**, because of either the nature of the work or the planned duration of the work package.

Performance specification* A statement of the totality of needs expressed by the benefits, features, characteristics, process conditions, boundaries and constraints that together define the expected performance of a **deliverable**.

Phase (of a project)* Part of a project during which a set of related and interlinked activities are performed to attain a designated objective. One of a series of distinct steps in carrying out a project that together constitute the **project life cycle**.

Phase reviews A review that takes place at the end of a life cycle phase. *See* **gate review**.

Physical models A representation of the three-dimensional, solid aspects of a deliverable which can be used to display its features or potentially test aspects of it.

Physical percent complete The percentage of the work content of an activity that has been achieved.

Physical performance Actual performance of work on a project that can be measured; for example, the number of drawings produced or lines of code written.

Pilot A form of testing a new development and its implementation prior to committing to its full release.

Plan An intended future course of action. *See* **project management plan**.

Planned activity An activity not yet started.

Planned cost* The estimated cost of achieving a specified objective. *See* **budgeted cost of work scheduled**.

Planning The process of identifying the means, resources and actions necessary to accomplish an objective.

Portfolio A grouping of an organisation's projects, programmes and related business-as-usual activities, taking into account **resource constraints**. Portfolios can be managed at an organisational, programme or functional level.

Portfolio management The selection and management of all of an organisation's projects, programmes and related operational activities, taking into account **resource constraints**.

Portfolio prioritisation process The evaluation and prioritisation of projects within a portfolio to enable the more important projects and programmes to access the required resources and to move forward in accordance with their plans.

Post-project review Undertaken after the project **deliverables** have been handed over and before final **closeout**, this review is intended to produce **lessons learned** that will enable continuous improvement.

Precedence diagram method A method of representing projects as networks, in which the activities are represented by nodes and the relationships between them by arrows.

Precedence network* A multiple dependency network. An **activity-on-node network** in which a sequence arrow represents one of four forms of precedence relationship, depending on the positioning of the head and the tail of the sequence arrow. The relationships are: *finish to start* – start of activity depends on finish of preceding activity, either immediately or after a lapse of time; *finish to finish* – finish of activity depends on finish of preceding activity, either immediately or after a lapse of time; *start to start* – start of activity depends on start of preceding activity, either immediately or after a lapse of time; *start to finish* – finish of activity depends on start of preceding activity, either immediately or after a lapse of time.

Pre-commissioning The work that is carried out prior to **commissioning** in order to demonstrate that commissioning may be safely undertaken.

Predecessor An activity that must be completed (or be partially completed) before a specified activity can begin.

Predecessor activity In the **precedence diagram method**, an activity that logically precedes the current activity.

Prime or lead contractor A main supplier that has a contract for much or all of the work on a contract. The prime contractor is responsible for managing projects that involve a number of subsystem contracts. It is responsible for coordinating the activities of subcontractors, integrating their **deliverables** and managing risks to meet the client's requirements.

PRINCE2 A project management method created for government projects, standing for PRojects IN Controlled Environments (second version). It is intended to be generic.

Private finance initiative (PFI) A form of **public–private partnership** by which the public and private sectors enter into a contract which shares between them the risk of undertaking an investment project, typically to provide a major capital asset for the public services, such as a school or a hospital, and related services such as repairs and maintenance.

Probabilistic network A network containing alternative paths with which probabilities are associated.

Probability The likelihood of a risk occurring.

Problems Concerns that the project manager has to deal with on a day-to-day basis.

Procedures Individual aspects of project management practice that form an integral part of a method.

Procedures manual A book of reference describing standard project procedures.

Process* A set of interrelated resources and activities that transform inputs into outputs.

Procurement The process by which the resources (goods and services) required by a project are acquired. It includes development of the **procurement strategy**, preparation of contracts, selection and acquisition of suppliers, and management of the contracts.

Procurement strategy A procurement strategy sets out how to acquire and manage resources (goods and services) required by a project.

Product *See* **deliverable**. (Note that in the **PRINCE2** method, product is used synonymously with deliverable.)

Product breakdown structure (PBS) A hierarchy of deliverables that are required to be produced on the project. This forms the base document from which the execution strategy and product-based **work breakdown structure** may be derived. It provides a guide for **configuration control** documentation.

Product description The description of the purpose, form and components of a product. It should always be used as a basis for acceptance of the product by the customer.

Product flow diagram A diagram representing how the products are produced by identifying their derivation and the dependencies between them. It is similar to a **network diagram** but uses products rather than activities.

Productivity factor The ratio of earned hours against expended hours.

Professional development *See* **continuing professional development**.

Professionalism and ethics In relation to proper conduct, professionalism is demonstrable awareness and application of qualities and competences covering knowledge, appropriate skills and behaviours; ethics covers the conduct and moral principles recognised as appropriate within the project management profession.

Profile of expenditure A project's budget is phased over time to give a profile of expenditure. This will allow a cash flow forecast for the project to be developed and a **drawdown** of funds to be agreed with the organisation.

Programme A group of related projects, which may include related business-as-usual activities, that together achieve a beneficial change of a strategic nature for an organisation.

Programme benefits review A review to assess if targets have been reached and to measure the performance levels in the resulting business operations.

Programme brief A description of the capability that the organisation seeks from changes to its business and/or its operations. Delivery of this capability is the end goal of the **programme**.

Programme director The senior manager with the responsibility for the overall success of the **programme**.

Programme directorate A committee that directs the **programme** when circumstances arise where there is no individual to direct the programme.

Programme evaluation and review technique (PERT) A project management technique for determining how much time a project needs before it is completed.

Programme management The coordinated management of related projects, which may include related business-as-usual activities, that together achieve a beneficial change of a strategic nature for an organisation.

Programme management office The office responsible for the business and technical management of a specific **programme**.

Programme manager The individual with responsibility for managing a **programme**.

Programme mandate What the **programme** is intended to deliver in terms of new services and/or operational capability.

Programme support office A group that gives administrative support to the **programme manager** and the programme executive.

Progress The partial completion of a project, or a measure of the same.

Progress payments Payments made to a contractor during the life of a fixed-price type contract, on the basis of some agreed-to formula, for example, **budgeted cost of work performed** or simply costs incurred.

Progress report A regular report to senior personnel, sponsors or stakeholders summarising the progress of a project including key events, **milestones**, costs and other issues.

Project A unique, transient endeavour undertaken to achieve a desired outcome.

Project appraisal The discipline of calculating the viability of a project. May be conducted at any time throughout the project.

Project assurance Independent monitoring and reporting of the project's performance and **deliverables**.

Project base date* *See* **base date.**

Project board *See* **steering group.**

Project brief* *See* **brief.**

Project budget *See* **budget.**

Project calendar *See* **calendar.**

Project champion* *See* **champion.**

Project charter *See* **charter.**

Project closure* *See* **closure.**

Project context The environment within which a project is undertaken. Projects do not exist in a vacuum, and an appreciation of the context within which the project is being performed will assist those involved in project management to deliver a project.

Project coordination* *See* **coordination.**

Project culture *See* **culture.**

Project director The manager of a very large project that demands senior level responsibility, or the person at the board level in an organisation who has the overall responsibility for project management.

Project environment *See* **environment.**

Project evaluation review A documented review of the project's performance, produced at predefined points in the **project life cycle.**

Project excellence model A model based on the **EFQM Excellence Model.** Developed in 1997 by the German Project Management Association and used as an evaluation tool to judge the annual German Project Management Awards.

Project file A file containing the overall plans of a project and any other important documents.

Project financing and funding The means by which the capital to undertake a project is initially secured and then made available at the appropriate time. Projects may be financed externally or funded internally, or there may a combination of the two.

Project initiation *See* **initiation.**

Project initiation document (PID) A document approved by the project board at project **initiation** that defines the terms of reference for the project. This document is similar and in some cases the same as the **project management plan** (PMP).

Project life cycle All projects follow a life cycle and life cycles will differ across industries and business sectors. A life cycle allows the project to be considered as a sequence of distinct phases that provide the structure and approach for progressively delivering the required outputs. *See* **concept, definition, implementation** and **handover and closeout.**

Project life cycle cost* *See* **life cycle cost.**

Project log* A project diary. A chronological record of significant occurrences throughout the project.

Project management The process by which projects are defined, planned, monitored, controlled and delivered so that agreed benefits are realised.

Project management body of knowledge *See* **Body of knowledge.**

Project management information system (PMIS) The systems, activities and data that allow information flow in a project, frequently computerised, but not always.

Project management maturity A model that describes a number of evolutionary levels in which an organisation's project management processes can be assessed, from ad hoc use of processes to continual improvement of its processes.

Project management plan (PMP) A plan that brings together all the plans for a project. The purpose of the PMP is to document the outcome of the planning process and to provide the reference document for managing the project. The project management plan is owned by the **project manager**.

Project management processes The generic processes that need to apply to each phase of the **project life cycle**. These may be described as a starting or initiating process, a defining and planning process, a monitoring and controlling process, and a learning or closing process.

Project management software Computer application software designed to help with planning and controlling projects.

Project management team Members of the **project team** who are directly involved in its management.

Project manager* The individual responsible and accountable for the successful delivery of the project.

Project mandate The initial terms of reference for the project – as defined in **PRINCE2**.

Project master schedule *See* **master schedule**.

Project network* A representation of activities and/or events with their interrelationships and dependencies.

Project objectives Those things that are to be achieved by the project, which usually include technical, time, cost and quality objectives, but may include other items to meet **stakeholder** needs.

Project office The office that serves the organisation's project management needs. It can range from simple support functions for the **project manager** to responsibility for linking corporate strategy to project execution.

Project organisation (structure) A means of providing maximum authority to the project manager. It provides integration of functional capabilities within projects. However, this leads to duplication of facilities and less efficient use of resources.

Project plan *See* **project management plan**.

Project planning The development and maintenance of a project plan.

Project portfolio *See* **portfolio**.

Project procedures manual *See* **procedures manual**.

Project progress report* *See* **progress report**.

Project quality management The discipline that is applied to ensure that both the outputs of the project and the processes by which the outputs are delivered meet the required needs of **stakeholders**. Quality is broadly defined as fitness for purpose or more narrowly as the degree of **conformance** of the outputs and processes.

Project review calendar* A calendar of **project evaluation review** dates, meetings and issues of reports set against project week numbers or dates.

Project risk The exposure of **stakeholders** to the consequences of **variation** in outcome.

Project risk management A structured process that allows individual **risk events** and overall **project risk** to be understood and managed proactively, optimising project success by minimising threats and maximising opportunities.

Project roles and responsibilities The roles and responsibilities of those involved in the project; for example, the sponsor and project manager.

Project schedule* The timetable for a project. It shows how project activities and **milestones** are planned over a period of time. It is often shown as a milestone chart, **Gantt chart** or other **bar chart**, or as a tabular listing of dates.

Project scope management *See* **scope management**.

Project sponsor *See* **sponsor**.

Project sponsorship An active senior management role, responsible for identifying the business need, problem or opportunity. The sponsor ensures that the project remains a viable proposition and that benefits are realised, resolving any issues outside the control of the **project manager**.

Project start-up The creation of the **project team** and making it effective.

Project status report A report on the status of accomplishments and any **variances** to spending and schedule plans.

Project steering group *See* **steering group**.

Project strategy A comprehensive definition of how a project will be developed and managed.

Project success The satisfaction of **stakeholder** needs measured by the **success criteria** as identified and agreed at the start of the project.

Project success criteria *See* **success criteria**.

Project support experts Individuals with expertise in particular aspects of project support such as scheduling, budgeting and cost management or reporting.

Project support office *See* **project office**.

Project team A set of individuals, groups and/or organisations responsible to the

project manager for working towards a common purpose.

Project variance Changes to cost or schedule that are within the current work plan or scope.

Public–private partnership (PPP) A generic term for the relationships formed between the private sector and public bodies, often with the aim of introducing private sector resources and/or expertise in order to help provide and deliver public sector assets and services. The term PPP is used to describe a wide variety of working arrangements from loose, informal and strategic partnerships to design, build, finance and operate (DBFO)-type service contracts and formal joint venture companies. The **private finance initiative** (PFI) is a form of PPP.

Public relations (PR) An activity meant to improve the project organisation's environment in order to improve project performance and reception.

Punch list A list of outstanding activities to be completed prior to final acceptance of the **deliverables**.

Qualitative risk analysis A generic term for subjective methods of assessing risks that cannot be identified accurately.

Quality The fitness for purpose or the degree of **conformance** of the outputs of the process.

Quality assurance (QA) The process of evaluating overall project performance on a regular basis to provide confidence that the project will satisfy the relevant quality standards.

Quality assurance plan A plan that guarantees a quality approach and conformance to all customer requirements for all activities in a project.

Quality audit An official examination to determine whether practices conform to specified standards or a critical analysis of whether a **deliverable** meets **quality criteria**.

Quality control (QC) The process of monitoring specific project results to determine if they comply with relevant standards and identifying ways to eliminate causes of unsatisfactory performance.

Quality criteria The characteristics of a product that determine whether it meets certain requirements.

Quality guide A guide that describes quality and **configuration management** procedures, aimed at people directly involved with **quality reviews**, configuration management and technical exceptions.

Quality management system The complete set of quality standards, procedures and responsibilities for a site or organisation.

Quality plan (for a project)* That part of the project plan that concerns **quality management** and **quality assurance** strategies.

Quality planning The process of determining which quality standards are necessary and how to apply them.

Quality review A review of a product against an established set of **quality criteria**.

Quantitative risk analysis The estimation of numerical values of the probability and impact of risks on a project usually using actual or estimated values, known relationships between values, modelling, and arithmetical and/or statistical techniques.

Rapid application development (RAD) A method of minimising the time necessary to complete development projects.

Reactive risk response An action or set of actions to be taken after a **risk event** has occurred.

Recurring costs Expenditures against specific activities that would occur on a repetitive basis. Examples are hire of computer equipment and tool maintenance.

Reduce To respond to a **threat** that reduces its probability or impact on the project, or both.

Regulatory A restriction due to the need to conform to a regulation or rule designed to control or govern conduct.

Reimbursement Method by which a contractor will be paid for the work undertaken.

Relationship A logical connection between two activities.

Remaining duration The time needed to complete the remainder of an activity or project.

Replanning Actions performed for any remaining effort within project **scope**.

Replenishable resource A resource that, if absent or used up, can be obtained in fresh supply. Raw materials and money are common examples. *See* **consumable resource**.

Reporting The presentation of information in an appropriate format which includes the formal communication of project information to **stakeholders**.

Reports Information presented in an appropriate format. Alternatively a written record or summary, a detailed account or statement, or a verbal account.

Request for change (RFC) A proposal for a change to the project.

Request for proposal (RFP) A bid document used to request proposals from prospective sellers of products or services.

Request for quotation (RFQ) Equivalent to a **request for proposal** but with more specific application areas.

Requirements A statement of the need that a project has to satisfy. It should be comprehensive, clear, well structured, traceable and testable.

Requirements definition* Statement of the needs that a project has to satisfy.

Requirements management The process of capturing, analysing and testing the documented statements of **stakeholder** and user wants and needs.

Reserve Like a contingency, the planned allotment of time and cost or other resources for unforeseeable elements within a project.

Residual value The written-down value of a capital item at the end of the period, used in the **business case** to assess the financial integrity of the **programme** or project.

Resource aggregation* A summation of the requirements for each resource, and for each time period.

Resource allocation* The process by which resources are mapped against activities which are often shown as aggregated resource histograms against a timescale.

Resource availability The level of availability of a resource, which may vary over time.

Resource calendar A calendar that defines the working and non-working patterns for specific resources.

Resource constraint* A limitation due to the availability of a resource.

Resource-driven activity durations Activity durations that are driven by the need for scarce resources.

Resource histogram A view of project data in which resource requirements, usage and availability are shown using vertical bars against a horizontal timescale.

Resource level A specified level of resource units required by an activity per time unit.

Resource levelling A process that can be applied to projects when there are **resource constraints**. Resource levelling forces the amount of work scheduled not to exceed the limits of resources available. This results in either activity durations being extended or entire activities being delayed to periods when resources are available. This often results in a longer project duration. It is also known as resource limited scheduling.

Resource limited scheduling *See* **resource levelling**.

Resource loading The amount of resources of each kind devoted to a specific activity in a particular time period.

Resource management A process that identifies and assigns resources to activities so that the project is undertaken using appropriate levels of resources and within an acceptable duration.

Resource optimisation A term for **resource levelling** and **resource smoothing**.

Resource plan A part of the **project management plan** that states how the project will be resource loaded and what supporting services, infrastructure and third-party services are required.

Resource planning A process that evaluates what resources are needed to complete a project and determines the quantity needed.

Resource pool The resources available to a project. Alternatively, a group of people who can generally do the same work, so they can be chosen randomly for assignment to a project.

Resource requirement The requirement for a particular resource by a particular activity.

Resource scheduling A process that ensures that resources are available when needed, and where possible are not underutilised.

Resource smoothing* A process applied to projects to ensure that resources are used as efficiently as possible. It involves utilising **float** within the project or increasing or decreasing the resources required for specific activities, such that any peaks and troughs of resource usage are smoothed out. This does not affect the project duration. It is also known as time-limited scheduling.

Resources All those items required to undertake a project, including people, finance and materials.

Responsibility assignment matrix (RAM) A diagram or chart showing assigned responsibilities for elements of work. It is created by combining the **work breakdown structure** with the **organisational breakdown structure**.

Responsibility matrix *See* **responsibility assignment matrix.**

Responsible organisation A defined unit within the organisation structure that is assigned responsibility for accomplishing specific activities, or cost accounts.

Retention A part of payment withheld until the project is completed in order to ensure satisfactory performance or completion of contract terms.

Reusable resource A resource that, when no longer needed, becomes available for other uses. Accommodation, machines, test equipment and people are reusable.

Revenue cost* Expenditure charged to the profit and loss account as incurred or accrued due.

Reviews Surveys that take place throughout the **project life cycle** to check the likely or actual achievement of the objectives specified in the **project management plan**.

Rework To repeat work already completed in producing a deliverable in order to remove defects and meet **acceptance criteria**.

Right first time Completing a deliverable which, on first testing, meets the agreed **acceptance criteria** with no defects and no rework required.

Risk* *See* **project risk** and **risk event.**

Risk analysis* An assessment and synthesis of the risks affecting a project to gain an understanding of their individual significance and their combined impact on the project's objectives.

Risk assessment The process of quantifying the likelihood of risks occurring and assessing their likely impact on the project.

Risk avoidance *See* **avoid.**

Risk breakdown structure (RBS) A hierarchical breakdown of the risks on a project.

Risk evaluation* A process used to determine risk management priorities.

Risk event An uncertain event or set of circumstances that, were they to occur, would have an effect on the achievement of one or more of the **project objectives**.

Risk exposure The degree to which a risk taker could be affected by an adverse outcome.

Risk identification* The process of identifying project risks.

Risk log A document that provides identification, estimation, impact evaluation and countermeasures for all risks to the project. It is normally maintained throughout the life of the project.

Risk management *See* project risk management.

Risk management maturity A measure of the extent to which a project or organisation formally applies effective risk management to support decision-making and the treatment of risk.

Risk management plan A document defining how risk management is to be implemented in the context of the particular project concerned.

Risk manager The person who is put in charge of matters connected with risk, or certain aspects of risk, on a project.

Risk monitoring The process of observing the state of identified risks (also referred to as risk tracking).

Risk owner The person who has responsibility for dealing with a particular risk on a project and for identifying and managing responses.

Risk prioritising Ordering of risks according first to their risk value, and then by which risks need to be considered for **risk reduction**, risk avoidance and **risk transfer**.

Risk ranking The allocation of a classification to the probability and impact of a risk.

Risk reduction Action taken to reduce the likelihood and impact of a risk.

Risk register* A body of information listing all the risks identified for the project, explaining the nature of each risk and recording information relevant to its assessment, possible impact and management.

Risk response An action or set of actions to reduce the probability or impact of a threat or to increase the probability or impact of an opportunity.

Risk response planning The planning of responses to risks.

Risk transfer A contractual arrangement between two parties for delivery and acceptance of a product where the liability for the costs of a risk is transferred from one party to the other.

Roll-out The process of delivering a number of nearly identical products to a number of users, usually after the product has been tested and shown to meet requirements.

Rolling wave planning The process whereby only the current phase of a project is planned in detail, future phases being planned in outline only. Each phase produces the detailed plan for the next phase.

S-curve A graphic display of cumulative costs, labour hours or other quantities, plotted against time. This curve tends to be flat at the beginning and end and steep in the middle, reflecting the lower expenditure of resources at the beginning and end of projects. It is usual to plot planned, actual and predicted values on the same chart.

Safety plan The standards and methods that minimise to an acceptable level the likelihood of accident or damage to people or equipment.

Sales A marketing technique used to promote a project.

Sanction Authorisation for the project or part of a project to proceed.

Schedule The timetable for a project. It shows how project activities and milestones are planned over a period of time. It is often shown as a milestone chart, **Gantt chart** or other **bar chart**, or as a tabular listing of dates.

Schedule dates Start and finish dates calculated with regard to resource or external constraints as well as project **logic**.

Schedule performance index (SPI) A term used in **earned value management**. It is the ratio of work accomplished versus work planned, for a specified time period. The SPI is an efficiency rating for work accomplishment, comparing work achieved to what should have been achieved at any point in time.

Schedule variance (cost) A term used in **earned value management**. The difference between the **budgeted cost of work performed** (or **earned value**) and the **budgeted cost of work scheduled** at any point in time.

Scheduled finish The earliest date on which an activity can finish, having regard to resource or external constraints as well as project **logic**.

Scheduled start The earliest date on which an activity can start, having regard to resource or external constraints as well as project logic.

Scheduling The process used to determine the overall project duration. This includes identification of activities and their logical dependencies, and estimating activity durations, taking into account requirements and availability of resources.

Scope The sum of work content of a project.

Scope change Any change in a project **scope** that requires a change in the project's cost or **schedule**.

Scope creep The term sometimes given to the continual extension of the scope of some projects.

Scope management The process by which the **deliverables** and the work to produce these are identified and defined. Identification and definition of the **scope** must describe what the project will include and what it will not include, i.e. what is in and out of scope.

Scope of work A description of the work to be accomplished or resources to be supplied.

Scope statement A documented description of the project that identifies the project boundaries, its output, approach and content. It is used to provide a documented basis to help make future project decisions and to confirm or develop a common understanding of the project's **scope** by **stakeholders**.

Scope verification A process that ensures that all identified project deliverables have been completed satisfactorily.

Secondary risk The risk that may occur as a result of invoking a **risk response** or fallback plan.

Sensitivity analysis An investigation of the effect on the outcome of changing parameters or data in procedures or models.

Sequence The order in which activities will occur with respect to one another.

Share To respond to an **opportunity** in a way that increases its probability or impact on the project, or both, by sharing the risk with a third party.

Simulation A process whereby some dynamic aspect of a system is replicated without using the real system, often using computerised techniques.

Six sigma A quality management programme to achieve 'six sigma' levels of quality. It was pioneered by Motorola in the mid-1980s.

Slack An alternative term for float. *See* **free float** and **total float.**

Slip chart A pictorial representation of the predicted completion dates of **milestones** (also referred to as a trend chart).

Slippage The amount of **float** time used up by the current activity because of a delayed start or increased duration.

Snagging The process of identifying minor small deficiencies that have to be rectified before acceptance of the work on a project or contract.

Social capital The pattern and intensity of networks among people and the shared values which arise from those networks.

Sole source The only source known to be able to supply particular equipment or services, or undertake a particular contract. It may be a source specified by the client for reasons not necessarily connected to the project.

Solicitation The process by which bids or tenders are obtained for the provision of goods or services to the project.

Source selection Choosing from potential contractors.

Spiral model A management model used particularly for development projects.

Splittable activity* An activity that can be interrupted in order to allow its resources to be transferred temporarily to another activity.

Sponsor The individual or body for whom the project is undertaken and who is the primary risk taker. The sponsor owns the business case and is ultimately responsible for the project and for delivering the benefits.

Stage A subdivision of the **project life cycle** into a natural subsection with well-defined **deliverables.**

Stage payment* A payment made part-way through a project at some predetermined **milestone.**

Stakeholder analysis The identification of stakeholder groups, their interest levels and ability to influence the project or **programme.**

Stakeholder grid A matrix used as part of a stakeholder analysis to identify the relative importance of **stakeholders** to a project; for example, by considering their relative power.

Stakeholder identification The process of identifying **stakeholders** in a project.

Stakeholder management The systematic identification, analysis and planning of actions to communicate with, negotiate with and influence **stakeholders.**

Stakeholders The organisations or people who have an interest or role in the project or are impacted by the project.

Start-to-start lag The minimum amount of time that must pass between the start of one activity and the start of its successor(s).

Start-up The formal process of making a new **project team** effective or the commissioning of a completed facility.

Start-up meeting The initial meeting with the **project team** at the start of a project or phase of a project.

Starting activity An activity with no predecessors. It does not have to wait for any other activity to start.

Statement of scope *See* **scope statement.**

Statement of work* (SOW) A document stating the requirements for a given project activity.

Status report A description of where the project currently stands, usually in the form of a written report, issued to both the **project team** and other responsible people on a regular basis, stating the status of an activity, **work package** or whole project. It may be a formal report on the input, issues and actions resulting from a status meeting.

Statute law The written law consisting of Acts of Parliament (including those enacted under European directives), and the rules, regulations and orders made under the powers conferred by those Acts.

Statutory approval An approval that is required by law.

Statutory obligations Relevant legal obligations.

Steering group A group, usually comprising the **sponsor**, senior managers and sometimes key **stakeholders**, whose remit is to set the strategic direction of a project. It gives guidance to the sponsor and **project manager**. Often referred to as the project board.

Strategy The high-level plan that will enable the project to reach a successful conclusion. It describes how the project is to be executed. This is the long-term plan.

Subcontract A contractual document that legally transfers the responsibility and effort of providing goods, services, data or other hardware from one firm to another.

Subcontractor An organisation that supplies goods or services to a supplier.

Subject matter experts Users with subject matter knowledge and expertise who may contribute to defining **requirements** and **acceptance criteria**.

Subproject A group of activities represented as a single activity in a higher level of the same project.

Success criteria The qualitative or quantitative measures by which the success of the project is judged.

Success factors Factors that when present in the project **environment** are most conducive to the achievement of a successful project. The success factors that if absent would cause the project to fail are sometimes termed critical success factors (CSFs).

Successor An activity whose start or finish depends on the start or finish of a predecessor activity.

Sunk costs Costs that are unavoidable, even if the project were to be terminated.

Super-critical activity A behind-schedule activity that has been delayed to a point where its **float** is calculated to be a negative value.

Supplier A contractor, consultant or any organisation that supplies resources to the project.

Supply chain management The management of the chain of organisations through which goods pass on their way from raw materials to the ultimate purchaser.

Surety An individual or organisation that has agreed to be legally liable for the debt, default or failure of a principal to satisfy a contractual obligation.

System The complete technical output of the project including technical products.

Systems analysis The analysis of a complex process or operation in order to improve its efficiency.

Systems engineering A systematic approach to realising a project that takes account of all related systems and subsystems.

Systems management Management that includes the prime activities of systems analysis, systems design and engineering, and systems development.

Talent management The development of project talented people in the organisation, each of whom is capable of filling a number of roles.

Target completion date The date planned to complete an activity or project.

Target start date The date planned to start work on an activity or the project.

Task The smallest indivisible part of an activity when it is broken down to a level best understood and performed by a specific person or organisation.

Team Two or more people working interdependently towards a common goal and a shared reward.

Team building The ability to gather the right people to join a **project team** and get them working together for the benefit of a project.

Team development The process of developing skills, as a group and individually, that enhance project performance.

Team leader The person responsible for leading a team.

Team member A person who is accountable to and has work assigned by the project manager to be performed either by the team member or by others in a working group.

Teamwork The process whereby people work collaboratively towards a common goal, as distinct from other ways that individuals can work within a group.

Technology management The management of the relationship between available and emerging technologies, the organisation and the project. It also includes management of the enabling technologies used to deliver the project, technologies used to manage the project and the technology of the project **deliverables**.

Tender A document proposing to meet a specification in a certain way and at a stated price (or on a particular financial basis), an offer of price and conditions under which a supplier is willing to undertake work for the client. *See* **bid**.

Tender document The document issued to prospective suppliers when inviting bids or quotations for supply of goods or services.

Tender list A list of approved suppliers to whom a specific enquiry may be sent.

Tendering The process of preparing and submitting a tender, quotation or bid.

Termination (phase) The disposal of project **deliverables** at the end of their life.

Terms and conditions All the clauses in a contract.

Terms of reference A specification of a team member's responsibilities and authorities within the project.

Testing The process of determining how aspects of a **deliverable** perform when subjected to specified conditions.

Theory of constraints A theory expounded by Goldratt which led to the **critical chain** schedule management technique.

Threat A negative risk; a risk that, if it occurs, will have a detrimental effect on the project.

Three-point estimate An estimate in which the most likely mid-range value, an optimistic value and a pessimistic, worst-case value are given.

Time analysis The process of calculating the early and late dates for each activity on a project, based on the duration of the activities and the logical relations between them.

Time-limited scheduling* *See* **resource smoothing.**

Time now* A specified date from which the forward analysis is deemed to commence. The date to which current progress is reported. Sometimes referred to as the status date because all progress information entered for a project should be correct as of this date.

Time recording The recording of **effort** expended on each activity in order to update a project plan.

Time sheet A means of recording the actual **effort** expended against project and non-project activities.

Time variance The scheduled time for the work to be completed less the actual time.

Time-boxing The production of project deliverables in circumstances where time and resources including funding are fixed and the requirements are prioritised and vary depending on what can be achieved in the time-box.

Top-down cost estimating The total project cost estimated according to historical costs and other project variables, and then subdivided down to individual activities.

Total float* Time by which an activity may be delayed or extended without affecting the total project duration or violating a target finish date.

Total quality management (TQM) A strategic, integrated management system for customer satisfaction that guides all employees in every aspect of their work.

Traffic light reports A type of progress report that explains the current status of the programme or project in the form of a traffic light colour: for example, red=problems, amber=some concerns, green=no problems.

Tranche A group of projects that represent the delivery of all or a recognisable part of a new capability. It is used to assist the management and control of a programme.

Transfer To respond to a **threat** in a way that reduces its probability or impact on the project, or both, by transferring the risk to a third party.

Trend chart *See* **slip chart.**

Trends A general tendency observed on a project.

Turnaround report A report created especially for the various managers responsible to enter their progress status against a list of activities that are scheduled to be in progress during a particular time window.

Turnkey contract A comprehensive contract in which the contractor is responsible for the complete supply of a facility, usually with responsibility for **fitness for purpose,** training operators, **pre-commissioning** and **commissioning.** It usually has a fixed completion date, a fixed price and guaranteed performance levels.

Uncertain event *See* **risk event.**

Uncertainty A state of incomplete knowledge about a proposition. Usually associated with risks, both threats and opportunities.

Unlimited schedule* An infinite schedule, a schedule produced without resource constraint.

User acceptance test A formal test or series of tests to demonstrate the acceptability of a product to the user.

User requirements The requirements governing the project's **deliverables** or products as expressed by the user. What the user needs expressed in user terminology.

User requirements statement A document that defines the user's needs in user terminology from the user's perspective.

Users The group of people who are intended to benefit from the project or operate the **deliverables**.

Validate To test that the **deliverable** meets the requirements.

Validation The process of providing evidence that a **deliverable** meets the needs of the user.

Valuation A calculation of the amount of payment due under the terms of a contract. Often undertaken at stages in large contracts and at completion.

Value A standard, principle or quality considered worthwhile or desirable. The size of a benefit associated with a requirement. In **value management** terms, value is defined as the ratio of 'satisfaction of needs' over 'use of resources'.

Value engineering In relation to optimising the conceptual, technical and operational aspects of a project's **deliverables**, a means of utilising a series of proven techniques during the **implementation** phase of a project.

Value management A structured approach to defining what value means to the organisation and the project. It is a framework that allows needs, problems or opportunities to be defined and then enables review of whether the initial **project objectives** can be improved to determine the optimal approach and solution.

Variance A discrepancy between the actual and planned performance of a project, either in terms of schedule or cost. Mathematical definition: the mean square difference between the value of all the observed variables and the mean (average) of all the variables – a measure of the spread and grouping of the distribution of a variable.

Variance at completion The difference between **budget at completion** and **estimate at completion**.

Variation A change in **scope** or timing of work that a supplier is obliged to make under a contract.

Variation order The document authorising an approved technical change or variation.

Vendor A company or person contractually committed to provide goods (either direct or through a supplier).

Verification Proof of compliance with specified requirements. Verification may be determined by test, analysis, inspection or demonstration.

Verify To test that the deliverable meets the specification and designs.

Version control The recording and management of the configuration of different versions of the project's products.

Virtual models A visual representation of a **deliverable** which can be used to test its operational performance.

Vision statement An outward-facing description of the new capabilities resulting from a project or **programme** delivery.

Warranty A promise given by a contractor to the client or owner regarding the nature, usefulness or condition of the supplies or services delivered under the contract.

Waterfall model A management model used particularly for IT development projects.

What-if assessment The process of evaluating alternative strategies.

What-if simulation* Changing the value of the parameters of the project network to study its behaviour under various conditions of its operation.

Work The total number of hours, people or effort required to complete an activity.

Work breakdown code A code that represents the 'family tree' of an element in a work breakdown structure.

Work breakdown structure* (WBS) A way in which a project may be divided by level into discrete groups for programming, cost planning and control purposes. The WBS is a tool for defining the hierarchical breakdown of work required to deliver the products of a project. Major categories are broken down into smaller components. These are subdivided until the lowest required level of detail is established. The lowest units of the WBS are generally **work packages**. In some instances work packages are further divided into activities that become the activities in a project. The WBS defines the total work to be undertaken on the project and pro-

vides a structure for all project control systems.

Work load The amount of work units assigned to a resource over a period of time.

Work package* A group of related activities that are defined at the same level within a **work breakdown structure**.

Work package manager A person with responsibility for leading and managing a part of a project to achieve specific aims that have been agreed with the **project manager**.

Work units The measurement units for resources. For example, people as a resource can be measured by the number of hours they work.

Working group A group of two or more people to whom work is delegated, with the interrelationships between activities managed through a single person who may be a member of the project team.

Yield The return on an investment.

Zero defects A measure of the quality of a deliverable where the deliverable is defect-free.

Zero float A condition where there is no excess time between activities. An activity with zero float is considered a critical activity.

PROJECT MANAGEMENT ACRONYMS

The following list details abbreviations and acronyms commonly used in project management across all sectors. Where an abbreviation or an acronym has more than one commonly used meaning, each project management-related meaning is given as a separate entry.

AC	Actual cost
ACWP	Actual cost of work performed
ACWS	Actual cost of work scheduled
ADM	Arrow diagram method
ADR	Alternative dispute resolution
ALAP	As late as possible
ALARP	As low as reasonably practicable
AOA	Activity-on-arrow
AON	Activity-on-node
APM	Association for Project Management
APMP	APM qualification at IPMA level D
ARR	Annual rate of return
ASAP	As soon as possible
B2B	Business-to-business
B2C	Business-to-consumer
BAC	Budget at completion
BCM	Business change manager
BCWP	Budgeted cost of work performed
BCWS	Budgeted cost of work scheduled
BoK	Body of knowledge
BOM	Bill of materials
BOOT	Build, own, operate, transfer
BOQ	Bill of quantities
BSI	British Standards Institution
CA	Configuration audit
CA	Control account
CAD	Computer-aided design
CAM	Computer-aided manufacturing
CAM	Cost account manager
CAPEX	Capital expenditure

CAPM	Certificate in Applied Project Management (PMI)
CB	Configuration board
CBS	Cost breakdown structure
CCB	Change control board
CCB	Configuration control board
CDR	Critical design review
CI	Configuration item
CM	Configuration management
CMM	Capability maturity model
CPA	Critical path analysis
CPD	Continuing professional development
CPI	Cost performance index
CPM	Certificated Project Manager (APM) – maps to IPMA level B
CPM	Critical path method
CR	Change request
CRD	Client requirements document
CSA	Configuration status accounting
C/SCSC	Cost/schedule control systems criteria
CSF	Critical success factor
C/SPCS	Cost/schedule planning and control specification
CTC	Contract target cost
CTR	Cost–time resource
CV	Cost variance
DCF	Discounted cash flow
DCP	Detailed cost plan
DRACAS	Defect reporting and corrective action system
DSDM	Dynamic systems development method
DSM	Design structure matrix
EAC	Estimate at completion
ECC	Estimated cost to complete
ECR	Engineering change request
EF	Early finish
EFQM	European Foundation for Quality Management
EFT	Earliest finish time
EMS	Environmental management system
EMV	Expected monetary value
EPC	Engineer, procure and construct
EPCC	Engineer, procure, construct and commission
EPIC	Engineer, procure, install and construct
EPMO	Enterprise project management office
ERM	Enterprise resource management
ES	Early start
ESA	End stage assessment
EST	Earliest start time
ETC	Estimate to completion
EU	European Union

EV	Earned value
EV	Expected value
EVA	Earned value analysis
EVM	Earned value management
EVMS	Earned value management system
FAST	Functional analysis and system technique
FAT	Factory acceptance test
FBOOT	Finance, build, own, operate, transfer
FCC	Forecast cost at completion
FEED	Front-end engineering design
FF	Finish to finish
FF	Free float
FFP	Fit for purpose
FMEA	Failure mode and effect analysis
FMECA	Failure modes, effects and criticality analysis
FS	Finish to start
FTE	Full time equivalent
GERT	Graphical evaluation and review technique
GoPM	Governance of project management
HAZCON	Hazardous condition
HAZOP	Hazard and operability
HRM	Human resource management
HSE	Health and Safety Executive
HSE	Health, safety and environment
IBR	Integrated baseline review
IC APM	Introductory Certificate Qualification
ICB	IPMA Competence Baseline
ID	Identification
IFB	Invitation for bidding
IPMA	International Project Management Association
IPR	Intellectual property rights
IPT	Integrated project team
IRR	Internal rate of return
IS	Information systems
ISEB	Information Systems Examination Board
ISO	International Standards Organization
IST	Integrated system testing
IT	Information technology
ITT	Invitation to tender
JIT	Just in time
JV	Joint venture
KISS	Keep it simple stupid
KM	Knowledge management
KPI	Key performance indicator
KRA	Key result area
LD	Liquidated damages

LFD	Late finish date
LOB	Line of balance
LOE	Level of effort
LOI	Letter of intent
LSD	Late start date
MIS	Management information system
MOC	Management of change
MoR™	Management of risk (OGC)
MPA	Major Projects Association
MR	Management reserve
MS	Milestone
MSP	Managing Successful Programmes (OGC)
MTO	Material take-off
NPV	Net present value
OBO	Operated by others
OBS	Organisational breakdown structure
OD	Original duration
ODC	Other direct costs
OGC	Office of Government Commerce
OPM3™	Organisational Project Maturity Model
OR	Operations/operational research
PBR	Programme benefits review
PBS	Product breakdown structure
PC	Planned cost
PDM	Precedence diagramming method
PDN	Project deviation notice
PDR	Preliminary design review
PDU	Professional development unit
PEP	Project execution plan
PERT	Programme evaluation and review technique
PESTLE	Political, economic, sociological, technical, legal, environmental
PF	Productivity factor
PFI	Private finance initiative
PID	Project initiation document
PIG	Probability-impact grid
PIM	Probability-impact matrix
PIR	Post-implementation review
PM	Project manager
PMB	Performance measurement baseline
PM BoK®	A Guide to the Project Management Body of Knowledge (PMI)
PMCDF	Project Manager Competency Development Framework (PMI)
PMI	Project Management Institute
PMIS	Project management information system
PMM	Project management maturity
PMMM	Project Management Maturity Model (OGC)
PMO	Project management office

PMP	Project management plan
PMP®	Project Management Professional (PMI qualification)
PMS	Project master schedule
PPP	Public–private partnership
PPR	Post-project review
PQ	APM Practitioner Qualification – maps to IPMA level C
PR	Public relations
PRAM	Project Risk Analysis and Management Guide
PRD	Project requirements document
PRINCE2	PRojects IN Controlled Environments
PROMPT	An early management methodology on which PRINCE was originally based
PSO	Project/programme support office
PV	Planned value
QA	Quality assurance
QC	Quality control
QMS	Quality management system
R&D	Research and development
RACI	Responsible for action, accountable (yes no decisions), consult before (2 way), inform after (1 way)
RAD	Rapid applications development
RAG	Red, amber, green
RAM	Responsibility assignment matrix
RAMP	Risk Analysis and Management for Projects
RBS	Risk breakdown structure
RCA	Root cause analysis
RFC	Request for change
RFI	Request for information
RFP	Request for proposal
RFQ	Request for quotation
RMP	Risk management plan
ROI	Return on investment
SCERT	Synergistic contingency evaluation and response/review technique
SD	System dynamics
SE	Systems engineering
SF	Start to finish
SHAMPU	Shape, harness and manage project uncertainty
SMART	Specific, measurable, achievable, realistic, time-framed
SOR	Schedule of rates
SOR	Statement of requirements
SOW	Statement of work
SPI	Schedule performance index
SS	Start to start
SSADM	Structured systems analysis and design methodology
SV	Schedule variance
SWOT	Strengths, weaknesses, opportunities, threats

Project management abbreviations and acronyms

TF	Total float
TLC	Through-life cost
TOR	Terms of reference
TQM	Total quality management
TSO	The Stationery Office
UAT	User acceptance test
VE	Value engineering
VM	Value management
VOWD	Value of work done
WBS	Work breakdown structure
WP	Work package